Mic

Why not be a missionary?

First published in 2000 by
the columba press
55A Spruce Avenue, Stillorgan Industrial Park,
Blackrock, Co Dublin

Cover by Bill Bolger
Origination by The Columba Press
Printed in Ireland by Colour Books Ltd, Dublin

ISBN 1 85607 298 3

Copyright © 2000, St Patrick's Missionary Society, Kiltegan

Contents

Preface	9
Comings and goings	11
Oldtimers	15
Incidentally	17
Invitation to study	19
Men in council	21
Page Two …	23
Man alive …!	25
Enter a stranger	27
Moment to remember	29
A thousand days	31
One night only	33
As having nothing and possessing all things	35
Look upon us	37
A street called Strait	39
A clean desk	41
Nobody is a nobody	43
Walk tall	45
On the move	47
Man in a jam	49
Scraping the barrel	51
Crazy, man!	52
Hating the children	54
Checking the price tag	56
Other cities	58
Knife twist	60
Value for time	62
The rights and wrongs of it	64
Today is full of things I want to do	66
Nobody you'd know	68
Stop fooling yourself	70
Crying out loud …	72
Fair-weather friends	74
The heart of the matter	76
Your witness	78
Men full grown	80

Taking for granted	82
High matters in a low key	84
The boss's eye	86
Friendship's risks	88
The edge of survival	90
Going for broke	92
Everything fixed	94
Pills in the garbage	96
The cutting edge	98
The frozen people	100
My face like flint	102
How safe is safe?	104
Fact and life	106
Lift the world's heart	108
Taking a tranquilliser	110
Sound and light	112
Send men to Joppa	114
The necessary average	116
Love constructs	118
Giving the treatment	120
Raise a shout	122
Breaking bread	124
Why not be a missionary?	126
Doing it my way	129
Holding hands	131
'Doesn't the thought of dying terrify you?'	133
Works and pomps	135
Wise old hard sayings	137
Measuring up	139
Six mile high	141
Read to the end of the story	143
Fame is – not – the spur	145
For this time only	147
… Over the hill	149
A great gospel	151
What's in a face?	153
A club to join	155
Buzz words	157
Who me?	159
What can I bring?	161
The real man	163

CONTENTS

Love in the morning	165
A Christmas *Yes*	167
No ifs and buts	169
More than the music	171
With open arms	173
Style	175
Consequences	177
Sending signals	179
The truth in love	181
For ever and a dream	183
The high ground	185
Irregular acquaintances	187
To nail it down	189
The insiders	191
High hearts	193
The narrow gate	195
A matter of principle	197
Pointing fingers and stiffening spines	199
Heading out – Is there a specifically missionary *thing*?	201
Mission accomplished	203
Flocks by night	205
When something like the moonflower happens	207
The bits of being good … one bit is being kind	209
The extra mile	211
Enough reality	213
Fr Michael Glynn	215

A word of thanks to
Mary D'Arcy, Josie Mulvany,
Fr Paddy Hyland and Fr Leo Sheridan
for their help in preparing this book.

Preface

During my final year at secondary school at Farranferris in Cork in 1963, and at a time when winning the Harty Cup in the Munster Schools' Hurling Championship was my consuming passion, I picked up a pamphlet entitled *Why not be a Missionary?* written by Michael Glynn. It consisted of a collection of articles extracted from *Africa* magazine. Most of these articles were addressed to a young man named John Smith and they invited and challenged him to do something valuable with the life God had given him. I read the pamphlet with growing interest. Each article was very readable and seemed to be written specially for me. It touched my youthful idealism and indicated to me that the life of a missionary priest was an attractive as well as a useful way to live. I became that John Smith.

Fr Michael Glynn died unexpectedly in August 1996. His final article in the *Why not be a Missionary?* series appeared in the September/October 1996 edition of *Africa* magazine, forty-four unbroken years after he wrote his first tentative piece in November 1952. Gary Howley, the current editor of *Africa*, has gathered together a collection of Michael's articles. They make fascinating reading. Though topical when written, they are not dated. They continue to be relevant because they move through the contemporary incident with which each article begins to the deeper and permanent realities of faith, hope, love and commitment. They engage the reader in a reflection, not just on life in general, but on the reader's own life and commitment; coaxing us to discern God's design in the ordinary events of our own everyday lives. These articles, written as vocation pieces, are stimulating and challenging for every Christian. After all, the call to be missionary is the vocation of every baptised person.

This collection is a tribute to Fr Michael Glynn from St Patrick's Missionary Society. I hope it will entertain, encourage and challenge all who read it.

Fr Seán Barry

Comings and goings

(November 1952)

A plane stoops down out of the sky away at the far end of the runway; the wheels touch and the tail drops gradually as it skims along the concrete towards you. This is the flight you've been waiting for. Things you hear from the family group near you on the balcony ... little excited half sentences ... give you to understand that this is the flight they've been waiting for also. Looking at them curiously as the plane manoeuvres to a stop on the parking apron, you discover resemblances to the traveller you're expecting. Well, you might have known that the family would be there ... this is something they've been looking forward to for years.

The stairway is adjusted and a hostess goes out, trim in her green uniform; and then the door of the plane is opened and the passengers file out, somehow hesitantly, into the sunlight. A girl in the group beside you cries out in a half whisper: 'There he is!'; and there he is indeed on the top of the ladder, taking his first look at the homeland through travel-dazed eyes. Another happy landing; and another missionary has come home. You know that he is shivering a bit in the unaccustomed cold; you know that he is desperately trying to adjust his mind to the sudden change of scene and circumstance. He'll be silent at the beginning and they'll wonder why he is so quiet ... and so restless. They won't realise that he is very much lost, very much out of touch and not a little homesick for the life and the people that have been his under another sky.

He has come a long way. Only yesterday or the day before, he was thousands of miles away, saying goodbye just about this time to the group of leave-takers on a green airstrip in East Nigeria ... two or three Fathers, a few tearful houseboys, children from the school. They'd have said, 'Father, God be with you,' ... 'Father, go, come,' ... and he'd have gone out to the little silver plane at the three strokes of the bell and strapped himself to the seat in the hot cabin, feeling lonely. He'd have had a few bad moments as they raced down the runway and climbed ... ever so slowly ... over the tops of the first palm trees. And then he'd have been looking down through the blue heat-haze, down at the endless forests, the small brown ribbons of the roads, the twisting creeks and the surf breaking on the shore along the gulf. Somewhere along the way he'll have gone searching frantically for his passport and found it pinned into his pocket ... the gold harp almost faded from the mottled green cover now after four years of damp and heat and mildew. He'll have read again, with a queer little excitement, the times on the flight schedule ... leaving Lagos at two in the afternoon, arriving London at nine in the morning; Aer Lingus plane from Northolt at three-thirty ... arriving Dublin, five-thirty. And in between the embarking and the arriving ... impressions, experiences ... camels at Kano with still, turbaned figures on their backs, night coming down over the long, brown reaches of the Sahara, landing in the crisp midnight chill of Tripoli, watching the flicker of lights down the length of the vast runways ... Italian waiters with cups of tea, British mechanics stripping the engines, an Arab with a hissing insect spray. He'd have awakened in the blue luxury of the cabin over the wing to see the dawn breaking gloriously over Sardinia and it would have been full day as they crossed the bay at Marseilles ... then the white towers of the clouds ... the unaccustomed feel of heavy black clothes. He'll have come down through the blind vapour and burst suddenly into glorious light over the incredibly green fields of Kent.

He's going to remember things afterwards. He'll remember the unbelievable kindness of the young men and women who work in airports and in aeroplanes, the shamrock flying at the top of a mast in Northolt and the friendliness of the Irish accents round about him inside the green Irish plane. And now this ... people waving to him from the balcony ... someone asking him to fill up a yellow form about foot-and-mouth disease ... the friendly, unhurried efficiency of Irish Immigration and customs officers ....

And so he comes through the barrier ... and you know, looking at the faces of parents and brothers and sisters, that this day is like no other day in history. For a moment you understand what it means to families to have a missionary member; what it means to them in heartbreak at his going and in loneliness while he remains away; what it means in happiness when he comes safely, just a bit worn, back to them ... and the insecurity of the happiness ... because he'll be going again. When you are a missionary you can be casual about your own going, for that is your life ... but where do families get the hardihood? ... who trains them to let you go and be without you? Now, for a flash you understand the heroism of those who remain and you are humbled and exalted all at once; and in your next prayer of thanksgiving for a missionary vocation you will include a thanksgiving for the vocation that came to your people also ... the vocation to be generous and self-forgetful, the vocation to be heroic when the heroism is stripped of natural consolation ... without the distraction of changing circumstance, the knowledge of achievement, the spice of adventure; the vocation to be content with hastily scribbled messages on crumpled airmail forms.

You think, for a moment, of the Irish missionary centuries ago, who had to step over the prostrate, protesting body of his mother, who did not wish to let him go – and you are thankful again ... for so many modern mothers who are more generous ... for so many families that are less demonstrative ... for the boundless goodness of God, pouring out in the sacrament of matrimony again and again the strength and the grace that's going to be needed in the years ahead when he will ask parents for their children.

It is evening at the airport and there is rejoicing. But there have been mornings there also ... mornings when you stood in the chill with someone going away. You helped him with his things at the weighing counter, said a cheerful last word and watched as he disappeared through the barrier. Afterwards there were brothers on the balcony, stiff-lipped watching the small silver speck pressing into the eastern sky. That is the other side ... the side you see too on evenings at this time of year down at the North Wall. It has become familiar now, but it still stirs you to see the *Munster* slipping out into the river and the line of waving missionaries along the rail. For some of them it's nothing new; for others it's the great adventure ... they will see the lights of Las Palmas like the lights of a fairy castle on the starboard beam next week, they will watch the flying fishes and the porpoises, lighthouses will flash their signals at night and passing ships salute by day ... and then one day they will rush to the rail to catch the first glimpse of Africa – a headland almost invisible in the haze where the sky and the sea meet. Going ashore in Gambia, in Takoradi, in Freetown, they will be solemnised to find God in a tabernacle ... and it may well be that as they set foot on land at their final destination, a bell will be ringing out the

Angelus ... a ringing that is the grandest welcome they could have wished for.

These are consolations ... but it is bleak on the North Wall for those who remain. And if a girl cries a little because her brother is gone ... who will blame her! If a boy is wordless and brusque because his sister is gone ... what does it matter! If parents, at home, are murmuring comfort to each other ... isn't it the most natural thing in the world! The blinding thing – the thing that is a glory around them – is the supernatural magnificence of their sacrifice. It is only in sudden brief flashes that the vision of this magnificence is vouchsafed to you ... but when it is – is it strange that you remember the cold-steel courage of the Mother of God ... watching her Son going down the road from Nazareth, a small figure in the distance going out from her to seek and to save?

Oldtimers

(September/October 1953)

One evening in 1951, the town of Calabar went mad – with delight. Someone whose memory the town had treasured for over twenty years was coming back on a visit. A brass band was at the wharf, as the launch came in, to play *Home Again*. A government car with the papal pennant flying on the bonnet was there to carry the visitor. Hilarious crowds found precarious standing room on the jetties and jammed the marine yard. As the car inched its way through the crowded streets, there were shouts of, *How-ell!* Up at the market square, the car stopped and the visitor alighted. The guard of honour came to the salute and up the whole length of the long street there rose a sound that could only be described as a sigh. It was then that Calabar went mad. Guard of honour, police, escort, everyone in the way – all were swept aside. Women danced round in circles. Everyone shouted and laughed and waved and shouldered. It was a triumphal procession, hysterically, childishly simple and joyful.

The centre of it all was a dignified old man with a white beard and a spring in his step, and he was the most joyful of them all. His slim, fragile figure, straight as an ash sapling, was garbed in a white soutane with a black girdle – the habit of a Holy Ghost Father on the missions. This was *How-ell*, the man whose name was a legend in Calabar town and bush, one of the most loved priests in Nigeria.

In the Cathedral he spoke to them and the voices of interpreters boomed his words in two languages to the packed thousands. 'Calabar was my first mission and I have always loved its people. I am so happy to come back ...' Big men and women from the town and bush broke down and cried. I think Father Howell cried too.

He didn't know it then, but it was a farewell visit. A few months ago, after more than forty years in Nigeria, Father Frank Howell died in Emekuku hospital. They buried him in Eze. Thousands of people lined the roads as his funeral passed and men and women came from Calabar and Ogoja to say goodbye.

To the St Patrick's Fathers, all still comparatively young, old Father Howell was more than just a missionary. He was almost the last link with the pioneer days, the days of Fathers McDermott and Lena and Crafft – the men who *opened* the Calabar Mission at the beginning of the century. He had set a standard of charity and zeal and dignity for all who came after him. In his person he had exemplified the reality of Christianity. Pagans had looked at him and seen – the Church. He was white and foreign, but it did not seem out of place to them to call him *Father*. He was one of those who broke the trail for St Patrick's Fathers. St Patrick's Fathers here salute the memory of a great missionary. It is not necessary to say more than *How-ell* – in Calabar that conveys everything we want to say about him.

Of the thousands who came to his funeral, who can say how many came to the faith, directly or indirectly, because he decided, back around 1900, to make the complete sacrifice of a missionary? How many souls of his own saving were waiting to greet him in heaven? How many will bring up the rear of his glorious and glorified escort? At the last day, we shall know. Meanwhile, might not you, perhaps, thinking on these things, find grace for the decision to do as he did and to be as he was!

Why not be a missionary?

Incidentally

(March 1954)

Let's suppose your name is John Smith. (Maybe it's not, but if you're a secondary schoolboy, this is addressed to you anyway.) Well, John Smith, we want to tell you two new stories from the missions and to ask you a question afterwards. Here is the first story:

'On the seventh of December, the children came to the mission to begin their thirty-day retreat in preparation for First Communion. On Wednesday, the sixth of January, they made their First Communion. They were all due back at school on the eleventh and *back to school* in Africa means a great deal of preparation: books to be got together, uniforms to be made, fees to be somehow raised, a food supply to be arranged in the case of boarders. But on Thursday morning none of them had gone home. They were all at Mass and Holy Communion. They were there on Friday morning again. I asked one of the seminarians that morning why the children did not go home. He had already asked them the same question. They told him: 'We have been a long time preparing to receive Our Lord and now that we have got him, we are not going to go away from him.' They were still in the mission on Saturday morning – and on Sunday. After Mass on Sunday, they went away reluctantly. They might not have a chance of receiving Our Lord again for a month or more.'

Now, the second story:

'December the fifth was a Saturday, and I opened the annual retreat for the members of the Legion of Mary in the evening. The Marian Year was to open on the following Tuesday, so on Sunday morning I told the people that we'd have a Solemn High Mass on Tuesday morning with a sermon on Our Lady. There was to be a curia meeting of the Legion on Monday at three. Just before it began, a message came from the bishop to say that the Vatican had cabled permission for a midnight Mass to usher in the Marian Year. It was, of course, too late to change the arrangements, but by way of impressing on the Legionaries the importance which the Holy See attached to the Marian Year, I told them about the permission. A little reflection – then someone asked: 'Why not have the midnight Mass for us?' I replied that I had made arrangements for a Solemn Mass next morning and it was too late now to let the people know about a change of plans. Whereupon I received the reply: 'Our Holy Father has given permission for midnight Mass to honour Our Lady. There is a special grace attached to carrying out the Holy Father's will. Please let us have the midnight Mass.' I went away to consult with the Father-in-Charge. He said: 'Have a Low Mass at midnight and Solemn High Mass in the morning as arranged.' The curia received this news with acclamation and great joy. It was five-thirty when the meeting was over, but the news went like wildfire through the villages. By ten o'clock the church was packed from the altar rails to the door and from that until midnight, rosary after rosary and hymn after hymn went up in gratitude to God for bestowing the privilege of the Immaculate Conception on Our Lady. Next morning the church (which is as big as a fair-sized cathedral at home) was crammed again. Someone had made a beautiful crown of moss and white flowers for the statue of Our Lady. I can't find out who did it, but Our Lady knows …'

The two incidents show a depth of faith and love that would be striking anywhere, but they both occurred in a place that, twenty years ago, was almost entirely pagan. We could reel you off a list of places that are still entirely pagan – places where things like these could happen if the people only got a chance.

So, John Smith – and here's your question –

Why not be a missionary?

Invitation to study

(January 1955)

Presuming that your motive is a good one, there are still three things you require in order to have a missionary vocation. The three things are health, holiness and knowledge. The first of these, health, is something you do not have to make any particular effort to acquire – it's given to you free. The other two, holiness and knowledge, come only by effort – your own effort – and the help of God. Let's pass over holiness this time and talk about something that is not so often discussed. Let's talk about knowledge – the knowledge that a missionary requires.

You've probably got the idea – it was once fairly common – that a missionary, because he works among simple, unlettered, pagan people, does not need to be *quite* as well educated as, say, a priest who works among races with centuries of culture behind them. Perhaps you're under the impression that something less than the best will *do* for the missions. But the Church has never said so; and the Church made no exception for missionaries when she prescribed, in her Code of Canon Law, the course of studies that must be taken by those who prepare for the priesthood.

As things stand, therefore, here is the situation. When you have finished your secondary course, you need never open a book to study again, *unless you choose to*. But, if you once decide to be a missionary, you no longer *have* a choice in the matter; you've just got to study. Because if you're going to be a priest that the Church won't be ashamed of, you're going to have to assimilate at least a certain well-defined *minimum* of information about such things as epistemology, ontology, cosmology, logic, psychology, ethics, natural theology, ascetical theology, moral theology, pastoral theology, dogmatic theology, canon law, sociology, missiology, catechetics, liturgy, and a variety of other things.

But *why?* Well, because this knowledge is standard equipment for a priest – just as anatomy, pathology, gynaecology, *et cetera*, are standard equipment for a doctor. How would you like to put your life in the hands of a doctor who does not know his business? And can you think of any good reason why people, pagan or otherwise, should be expected to entrust their chances of eternal life to a priest who lacks the knowledge to guide them with safety and certainty? A priest ignorant of the sacred sciences would be as great a menace to the souls of men as a surgeon who did not know his anatomy would be to their bodies.

If the needs of the missions at a particular time happen to demand it, you are liable, in addition, to be asked to take a degree in a *secular* subject, such as arts, science, music, economics, civil law; assuming, of course, that you have the aptitude and the ability. A young, growing Church requires the most surprising *special* equipment in her ministers from time to time. Just now a St Patrick's priest is spending his leave from the missions learning how to dissect biological specimens. It is his own idea; no one asked him to; he just found that he'd be a more effective missionary in his particular work if he knew something about dissection. Another missionary on leave is learning the secrets of the complicated machinery of the printing trade. A third is studying the composition of soil, the uses of fertilisers, the handling of livestock.

Well, you see we're being straight with you. Not for a moment would we attempt to conceal from you that our invitation to you to be a missionary involves and implies an invitation to be a student; an invitation to study. Perhaps you are the type that enjoys study, or perhaps you are not. But there's this to remember: a missionary does not study just for the sake of studying. He studies for the salvation of souls, for the advantage of the Church, for the glory of God.

Because, don't forget – you are a missionary from the first day you sign on; you don't have to wait till you're out under the sun with the palm trees around you. Studying at a desk in Kiltegan and trekking the forest trails of Nigeria are, equally, part of the job. The years of study are no more years of merely *waiting* than were the thirty years the greatest missionary of all spent in his carpenter's shop.

Why not be a missionary?

Men in council

(January 1956)

Now that the road has evened out a bit, the milestones come up quicker, eighty ... seventy-nine ... seventy-eight ... seventy-seven ... then another bad patch and a full hour of wrestling the car through the mud, reversing, digging out, crawling, before seventy-six comes in sight. Just beyond the junction at milestone thirty, an urgent horn-blast from behind calls for the road. You ease to the side and a mud-caked jeep sweeps by through the narrow gap between you and the cliff-face. 'Fág an bealach!' a voice shouts. The jeep slews to the left, brake lights flickering a warning, and stops. You hear the rasp of its handbrake ratchet. You switch off, your front bumper one inch from the tail bumper of the jeep.

A red head appears at your window, helmet pushed back. 'This is a hold-up! Yer money or yer life!' the red head says. You laugh. 'It's all yours, bandit – plus six hundred of an overdraft.' You shake hands, studying each other to see what changes six months have made. Suddenly the mountain road is no longer lonely. In silence, warm with companionship, you look out together for a timeless minute across the rift. You share the impact of the shattering drop to the valley floor, and squint against the sun up the towering face of the cliff. No need to talk. These mountains, that valley, the heady sky, have the same effect on both of you. Their fascination is a shared thing.

You shrug it off. 'That jeep,' you say, 'is the nicest sight I've seen for one hundred and forty miles. I'll take a lift with you. I'm tired.' You leave the car at a farm down the road, and climb in with him. You gloat: 'This saves me two gallons of petrol, and maybe a back spring. Keep your own side of the road, will you!' You settle down to *back-seat-drive* with relish. 'You couldn't possibly ram her into another pothole or two? The Lord is kind – another corner like that and we'll be over the side and – down, down, down. Well, we won't die without the priest, neither of us.' Something raps you smartly on the back of the head. You look. A dead buck is lying on the back seat, four upstretched legs swiping grotesquely to the lurch of the jeep. You pat the smooth hide. 'Poor Rudolf,' you say. 'He hit you when you weren't looking, I bet.' Red head boasts: 'One barrel, my friend, only one barrel fired from a moving vehicle – and he on the run too.' 'And your guardian angel driving it?' 'With the help of my left elbow! Anyway,' he says, 'your poor Rudolf will help to feed the troops down at Number One. The good mountain meat that puts brawn in a mission.' He flexes a stout arm to demonstrate.

Into the streets now. Into the mission compound, where the battered, mud-covered boneshakers of the earlier comers stand ranged, faced for the road. 'What's for the larder?' the welcoming host asks the red head, who makes a habit of this. 'Item, one buck, fresh ... that'll cost you some sugar and coffee, brother. I'm run out of both.' 'I know,' ruefully from the host. 'You always are. Well, let's get him to the kitchen before he rots!'

Prayer, together, in common, washed and changed, and serious now. Then to the conference, deadly serious and earnest. Twenty men, pooling experience and ingenuity, pitting themselves against the appalling problems of their vast territory. A man paces the floor as he talks, another reclines quietly on the arm of a chair; someone raps out a pipe on the heel of his shoe; someone interjects quiet wisdom from a corner, where he sits on the floor fondling the head of the mission dog. Bulking large against the door-jamb, head touching the lintel, the leader throws in a question, sometimes announces a thoughtful decision, mainly listens. Someone tells a yarn, true, unvarnished, illustrating a ludicrously desperate situation on his mountain. The seriousness splits wide open in laughter. Nothing looks so desperate after you've laughed at it. Decisions are taken; the grounds of new policy laid. Yes, try this, try that ... try anything, try everything that the united solidarity of us all can provide, to break down the barriers, to make a road for God.

You load up with provisions at the shops and head back into the hills. The milestones come up, fast or slow, seventy-seven ... seventy-eight ... seventy-nine ... crawling, slithering, fighting the wheel. Warmed by the late companionship, still relishing the solidarity of twenty men in close league for the soul of the mission's thousands, you are not lonely, small though you are and alone against the vastness of the rift.

        Why not be a missionary?

Page Two ...

(February 1956)

Hello John Smith! Here, once again, is your *Page Two* pep talk on *being a missionary*. With a difference, though. Beside the typewriter on which this is being written, there lie (awaiting consignment to the wastepaper basket) twelve sheets of foolscap-size paper, all covered with fairly accurate double-spaced type. And all scrapped! That represents several hours' work on the part of the missionary who writes this page, also a good deal of thought and a goodish lot of frustration. This month, ideas (and some of them good ones) have simply refused to take the right twist. The twelve rejected pages are about as easy to read as the small print in a German theology book. And that won't do. Above all things, this page has got to be readable. Meanwhile, the printer is waiting for the material for the February issue of *Africa*, and he can't wait very much longer – so we're sending him this!

We're not so far off the point, though, as you might expect. We are, you'll notice, talking about just one other aspect of the life of a missionary. It's probably never occurred to you to think about it – but how do you suppose this magazine gets prepared every month? Someone, naturally, has to prepare it. Someone has to plan it months ahead, every line, every word, every picture. Someone has to see that it's printed ... and that it gets to its readers. *Page Two* is only *one* of the pages that can be difficult once in a while! Well, it's a job that some missionary has to be responsible for – even though it was maybe the last thing in his head when he signed on, at your age, to work for the pagans.

But let's talk about this *Page Two!* This particular page is intended for John Smith, and John Smith is any boy who is eligible to be a missionary priest – in other words, *you*. It's rather likely that you have seen that prayerbook picture of an angel-faced boy in a collar and tie with the shadowy figure of Christ bending over him and whispering in his ear. The title as far as we remember is, *Follow Me!* The picture is all very well in its way, but the John Smiths of the world are not usually – at least the ones that eventually come to Kiltegan – angel-faced at all! And Christ doesn't, in the normal way, say, 'Follow me,' into any boy's ear like that. If he did, the issues would be very clear-cut. It would be merely a question of the boy's saying, 'Right, Lord, I will,' or, 'No, Lord, I won't.'

But the John Smiths of the world know that it is not quite as simple as that. Some of them, at least, could tell you that it is quite difficult to make up your mind on this question of *vocation*. Oh yes, one boy was born to be a missionary, and he knows it, and he has never contemplated being anything else. But another (with just as good a vocation) is torn asunder by many different attractions. He looks with reverence on his parents' lives, on the home they've made and the family they've reared, and he loves the idea of spending his life as they spent theirs. Or the missions call out to something big in him, but he's paralysed by a sense of unworthiness (based, perhaps, on slips, weaknesses, errors, in his past). Or he's appalled by the possibility that he may turn back when already he has put his hand to the plough. Or he's confused by the attraction of such things as making a name for himself, developing some unusual talent, being a surgeon, or a farmer. Or he's got exaggerated notions about the physical fitness required in a missionary. Or there's some difficulty about money – and he's as secretive about it as if it were a crime. Or he happens to like dancing. Or he worries his head off because he's not repelled by girls as a class or by a particular girl as a person! Oh, it can be complicated enough. We don't overlook that. After all, once upon a time, we had our own difficulties.

That's why we write *Page Two* for John Smith. Maybe it helps to sort out his tangles. Maybe not. We don't know. We just send it out into the blue and hope that it does help. We touch on most of the problems from time to time. Have we discussed yours? No? Well, you can always remind us. A note from you to *Page Two*, St Patrick's, Kiltegan (signed or unsigned as you please) might bring a most welcome and useful suggestion for the subject matter of this page; might give us another bracket on which to hang the question:

Why not be a missionary?

Man alive …!

(January/February 1957)

When you're seventeen … eighteen, nineteen … and decide to be a missionary, you're in no mood for haggling or bargaining. You're in the mood *to give*. You are in the state of mind when the most important thing in the world is to get your boats burned behind you. You want to give yourself, and you want to give everything you've got, without weighing the greatness or littleness of what you're giving. Of course it is a big thing you're doing, and you're not expected to be such a complete fool that you will be unaware of that – but seen against the powerful beauty of your ideal, your own decision doesn't seem all that important.

The fact is, you're ready for anything, now that you have decided that it's to be all or nothing. You'll take hardship if need be, and you'll take privation. You'll take sickness and persecution, and sudden death, if that's laid out for you. And you'll take work, work, work, and like it. And if a small doubt smoulders somewhere deep in your mind as to whether you are made of the stuff that these things call for, you'll quiet it with the thought that others made of the same stuff as you have given a good account of themselves … so why not you? It is a fine brave generosity that the Lord gives when he gives the grade for the primal decision to be a missionary.

But pause a bit. See the whole picture. You may indeed have privation, and work you will have surely. You will take your share – and maybe more than your share – of the burden of the day and the heats. You *may* die young, and gloriously – even violently – who can tell? But while it is a good thing to be geared for these things, it is also a good thing and a prudent thing to face the possibility that you will live to be a hundred and get rheumatics.

For that *is* a possibility. Leaving aside such unpredictables as persecutions, the life expectancy of a modern missionary is probably as high as that of any profession at home or abroad. In the course of duty, in defence of a principle, in confession of his faith, a missionary may, indeed, be called upon to give his life. But that is, after all, exceptional. In the normal way, what is demanded of him is not that he give his life – but that he should *live* it. *And live it as long and as usefully as he can.*

To throw away life or health recklessly, to take foolish and unnecessary risks, is no service to the Church. On the missions, overwork is sometimes unavoidable, and one takes a risk when one cannot avoid it ... but the missionary, like a sensible man anywhere, takes – and is bound to take – as much care as he can to preserve life and health for the longest and most fruitful possible span of time. If he works in a bad climate, he is pulled out of it at regular intervals (whether he likes it or not), so that his resistance to disease may have a chance to build up. If he is under prolonged strain ... responsibility, debt, loneliness ... it is less expensive to relieve him *before* he cracks than to *mend* him afterwards. He will go back to work much more vigorously after a rest than after a convalescence.

When you are wrapt up in the activity of a developing mission parish, or absorbed in some half-completed scheme for the expansion of the Church, it can be – and frequently *is* – a greater sacrifice to down tools and take a holiday than to carry on with the job. Even on an ordinary day, with holidays far-distant, taking time off for reasonable recreation often makes greater demands on one's obedience and common sense than working overtime. But a missionary is expected to take the long view, and to stay alive and active as long as he can; because – if you want just one reason – missionaries are scarce, and not easily replaced.

Why not be a missionary?

Enter a stranger

(March 1958)

You meet a young man on the path near the mission and his tight-lipped smile has a hidden, puzzling quality. You pass the group lounging near the market, and though they give the customary greeting, you notice the wry smiles they exchange among themselves. You go to the church to give the Sunday evening Benediction, and there's nobody there – practically nobody, just the faithful few you find even in the worst of places, the staunch ones you don't have to worry about. Nobody at the instruction classes in the evenings. A half empty church at Sunday Mass. You twiddle your thumbs at confession time – nobody coming.

And you're worried. You're new here. Only a month gone by you parked your loads and worked your way by lorry and ferry to take up this appointment. Nobody showed any interest, much, in your arrival at the empty mission – though you saw the covert glances exchanged at the crossroads as you stopped to enquire the way.

Oh yes, you're worried. This place has a chip on its shoulder. There's an indefinable aloofness about it, a sort of studied reserve, almost amounting to hostility. And this place shouldn't be like that. It's one of the old parishes, Catholic by tradition – one of the places that grasped the faith with the two hands fifty years ago when the old French Fathers tramped into the village and sat down to reason things out with chiefs and people. Here is none of your raw paganism, where a man might get down to work looking for conversions. Here is none of your virgin soil. This place has been ploughed over and the seed has sprung and the fruit has been gathered again and again in rich harvests. So what's wrong – and what are you going to do about it?

You sit down wearily under the hissing pressure lamp in the mission at night and read your way through the logbook – through fifty years of terse entries that give you the history of a mission parish. And when you finish your reading, you look into vacancy for a long time ... because you've found what's wrong, but you do not know yet just what you are going to do to put it right.

You're just another stranger here, and this place has had too many strangers in the mission-house ... priests it didn't get to know, because they weren't left long enough. Seven changes in two years – and before that, back a bit, two full years of a complete close down because there wasn't a priest to send. Well, you couldn't expect the people to like it. For fifty years they had stood firm. Loyal and faithful through thick and thin – and it was mostly thin! You give them a priest, and after three months you take him away from them. And why? Where do you send him? You send him to some place where the need is greater, very much greater. You replace him just as soon as you can. Well the change was necessary – but it left a hurt. Nobody likes to be treated as of less importance than another.

Trouble was, of course, that the danger points were in other places. This mission, for the moment, was reasonably secure. It was out in the far bush, a long way from the big centres of population, from the places you *had* to win a foothold in quickly if you weren't to lose them – and more along with them – for ever. This place would carry on somehow on the strength of its traditions till men could be spared to give it the real attention it deserved. Meanwhile – the battle was elsewhere, and the faith of the old bush mission was protected by its isolation if by nothing else. If there had been enough priests, this neglect would never have occurred.

But it *did* occur – and here *you* are now to bring back what neglect has taken away. You're a stranger. You're not very popular. You're lonely. And every man, woman and child in this place is watching you and waiting for a chance to obstruct you, just to work off a resentment that has been years building up. So you'll take things easy for a bit till they get used to having you among them, and you'll close your eyes to indifference and you'll ignore all the pinpricks, and you'll have the soft word on your lips always. And you'll spend a long time on your knees looking for the patience and the suavity you'll be needing. And you'll visit the compounds – unwelcome though you are – until you've broken down the barriers; until, some weary evening, some man puts a chair behind your knees and puts food before you, and you eat the token meal, breaking the bread of reconciliation in their fashion.

All this is not going to be a bit easy and you are not going to enjoy the months ahead. But all this is your job — a missionary's job.

Why not be a missionary?

Moment to remember

(December 1958)

You will remember this moment always. You will remember how the small boy stood, not too much at his ease, and the tone of his voice as he asked the question. And you will remember how it was that evening, how the twilight melted into the dark as you talked, how the smoke spiralled from the little cooking-fires in the compounds round the mission, how the sound of a band came up to you distantly from a street in the lower levels of the town. How he said: 'I know about all that; I am not afraid,' … and how your heart lifted up out of its forlornness …

You had been hearing confessions for Christmas; three or four days sitting in the heat. The long lines of people waiting came to an end at last. You waited a bit. The stragglers came. Finally, there was no one left, and you went out of the hot church to get what air there was. Inevitably, you met some latecomers outside. You went back into the church. You went out again – and there were more latecomers. Finished for the third time, you waited a little to see if there would be more, decided that they were at last really finished, come out again, and met three others hurrying – now they were *all* finished. You sank down on the church steps, aware suddenly that you were utterly tired, drained of the will ever to stand up on your feet again; and then that strange forlorn feeling, neither loneliness nor discontent, descended on you, as it sometimes will when prolonged effort ceases and there is, for the time being, nothing to do.

So far, a normal Christmas Eve. A rest here in the short twilight, a cold shower, a change of clothes, some food – and you'd have forgotten the tiredness and be braced again for action; the midnight Mass, the morning bush-stations, the endless communions, the blazing Christmas heat.

You regarded the small boy a little warily when he came. He might just be the latest of latecomers for confession. He might, with that peculiar African genius for choosing the incongruous moment, be coming to make any one of a thousand unwelcome requests. He might be the bearer of a message that would snatch from you this half-hour of hard-won leisure. He might have decided that you were lonely and come in the thoughtful African way to keep you company. But this particular small boy usually meant trouble when he came, for whatever mischief went on among the boys in the school, *this boy* would be up to his neck in it.

This time, it was not mischief. He gave the greeting and paused irresolute. Then shyness came down on him and you had to wait a long time before he spoke. And when he spoke, he said: 'Will Father please tell me what I must do in order to become a priest?' So you told him, not glamourising it; leaning, in fact, towards the other extreme, testing his mettle. And already your casual questions were probing, trying his motives, filling out his background. Already the scrutiny of his suitability, his fitness, his character, was beginning; and that careful examination would go on until he was as old again as he was now – thirteen years, perhaps fourteen – he'd be twenty-six or twenty-seven if he persevered, you reckoned, by the time he reached the priesthood. But here he was, ready to start – and here were you, satisfied that this was good material, ready to give him his start.

You will always remember that Christmas Eve … how the band played down in the town and the sound of roistering and revelry, the games, the dances and the plays, came up to you. You'll remember how a small boy was so preoccupied with his new ambition that he forgot, for the moment, to be either merry or mischievous. You'll recall how happy that particular Christmas was for you, how the whole festivity was coloured by the blinding thing that was happening in the soul of a small boy. When you remember, you will close your eyes for a moment and pray … oh, for many a year yet, for he is still but half-way on the rugged course … you will pray that, knowing now better than then what he is facing, he may still have the hardihood to say: 'I am not afraid.' And then, one Christmas, if God be kind, you will kneel at his feet while he blesses you …

Why not be a missionary?

A thousand days

(November 1959)

Little black fingers trace the path of the letters on the smooth limestone slab sometimes when small children hold informal spelling lessons at the grave. We don't tell them to stop, and we don't drive them away. It is the last thing *he* would have dreamt of doing. And, anyway, they never go away without getting on their knees and beaming their small powerful prayers on the Almighty.

We hardly ever read the writing ourselves. We know all it can tell us, and a lot more. But we do sometimes contemplate the design of vine-leaves with the chalice and the crossed stole which is carved on the stone. It answers a question for us, and it puts heart into us.

You could hardly say he died suddenly, but it was sudden enough. One night he was there, a member of the team, tamping tobacco with his pipe in that urgent kind of way he had, saying his word and making his comment as usual, while we tossed the day's problems and the morrow's plans back and forward to one another across the supper table. And that night, a week after, we were there without him, our talk coming heavily out of long silences. It was as sudden as that, if you call it sudden.

We laid him there in the sunny compound, right in the middle of things. There's the chapel nearby, and the long lines of the schools, the grapefruit and orange trees loaded with fruit, and the palm forest pressing in all round the verges. It's not a quiet place. All day you have the seething undertone of the big market down the road.

Myriads of children fill the day with their voices, chorusing their lessons in the schools, singing off prayers and catechism – and making holy bedlam at playtime. All night you have the drums, whispering, murmuring, lamenting, exulting, thundering, out in the bush. You have wild harmonies coming from a dozen points round the forest – and the *Salve Regina* trembling in sheer beauty through the compound for a few lovely minutes as our crack men's choir sings goodnight to Our Lady. No, it's not a quiet place, but it has its own kind of peace. He was happy here.

If you have the know-how, you can play our mood on a drum, as you can on a piano or a violin. When he died, the drums were strong and sad at night. The people had known him in all the bush villages. They were lonely. They played loneliness on the drums. The strong slow beat, stopping abruptly in the middle of a rhythm-pattern – it nearly broke our hearts. When you get to know the drums, they have a way of talking to you. The abrupt stopping of the beat was like a question mark. It said: Why did he die? – he was so young – and what do we do now?

Well, we carried on. You have to. You have to learn to live with a loss. He was a mighty loss. He had everything – enthusiasm, drive, energy, initiative, imagination, holiness. They didn't come any better. We knew we couldn't spare him. Apparently God knew better. A lifetime of preparation – for only three years of active campaigning: did it make sense? We tried to see it. It had made sense for God's own Son – so – our man was twenty-eight.

How much can a missionary achieve in three years? The carving on the cross reminds us of one achievement – the Mass. Three years is more than a thousand days. How do you reckon the value – or the effects – of the thousand Masses he celebrated during his brief span, in the crude shelters in outlandish places through the forest and along the rivers? That's his personal achievement as a priest. And then, sacraments, how many confessions, communions, extreme unctions, baptisms, marriages? No one knows – up in the high thousands – that's as close as you can reckon. A man loses count quickly when all his days are full of pouring out grace.

As regards other things – in these missions you don't write anything down to the individual; everything is a team-job, where one man sows and another man reaps. But when a man has pulled his weight, it cannot be hidden. This man pulled his weight, and we don't need the laconic entries he penned in the station logbooks, or the pages of entries in his hand in the parish registers, to tell us that. The thing that hits us all the time is that his work is not *finished*. It never will be. We have extra work to do because he got this and that going and because it has grown and developed. We have extra stations to visit because he founded them. We reap where he has sown. The reaping of his fruits goes on. It will go on – and long after we have joined him in his rest in that sunny plot in the compound.

Why not be a missionary?

One night only

(December 1959)

You round the last bend of the narrow path between the trees, wiping the sweat from your face. As you come in sight of the village, a bell begins to ring. It is the signal – the priest has come. Out on the farms, they will begin to gather up their tools and hasten homewards. People on the way from market will put an extra inch onto their stride. Children will leave their play. The priest has come. He does not come often. They will drop everything and hurry. As you march up to the rest-house, you know that you have, perhaps, half an hour to clean up and get ready for them.

The livingroom of the little rest-house is doorless, open to the day. You duck under the hanging thatch of the verandah and take a quick look round inside. Someone has swept the floor, but overlooked a great cobweb with enormously strong strands which reaches across a corner at face level. You walk into it before you notice, and it grips you across the eyebrows like a strip of sticking plaster. The roof is sound enough, though the sky shows through in one place, where the mats have parted. In a corner of the small inner room the wall is beginning to crumble. You try to remember – can it be? – yes, it is! – over six years since you opened a Mass-station here and got them to build a rest-house. Seven years, more or less, is the life of a mud-house. This one has about *had it,* but it will serve a turn yet.

Your eyes travel slowly, square by square, along the criss-crossing/bamboo roof-laths under the thatch, searching … there are no snakes; then up and down the rolling hand-patted surface of the mud walls … there is no squat still patch of black that might be a centipede. There are no ant-trails near the door. And this is not scorpion country. The rest-house is habitable and free of pests. You call out, and the carriers come in, one by one, and lay down their head-loads on the empty floor … bedroll, duffle-bag, chop-box, cooking outfit, Mass-box … check – everything correct. Here now comes someone with the loan of a table and a kitchen chair from a neighbour's house. Put the table down in the middle of the floor. Sit down gratefully on the upright chair. And you're home again!

Home again ... today, yesterday, tomorrow ... home for one night only, to one or other of fifty rest-houses in the bush, one like the other, each with its two rooms, each with its bathroom at the back – a three-by-three shelter without a roof, four tall fencing mats for walls and a gravelled floor for soakage – where, with two buckets of water you can get clean after the hot dusty journey of the day. Home! Not indeed a conventional home, with deep-seated comfort and a lifetime's accumulation of beloved trivia, but (three weeks out of the month) the only home a bush-trekking missionary knows – or wants to know. Not luxurious, but adequate, with living reduced to its simplest, its essential terms ... a shelter for the night, an address where (everybody knows) you can be found for sick calls, a place where, for this one-night stop, you are available to everyone, Christian or pagan, who wishes to make use of you on the narrow path to God.

They are coming now, you hear their voices, glad, excited voices. It is a time for gladness. Tonight the *priest* is in the station. The Father is with his children. Tonight there is forgiveness of sin, the richness of outpouring grace, God's word preached, the promise of salvation held out yet again. Tonight a man may come like Nicodemus, seeking a sign to put his doubts and fears at rest. And tomorrow – tomorrow, for the brief beautiful hour of the Mass, the Saviour himself will be in the station. He will enter the yearning hearts starved for the Eucharist. Then, for a month or more, till the priest can come again, they must strengthen themselves on the lingering sweetness of that banquet.

Tomorrow, the priest must go. Their eyes will follow you, lonely orphaned eyes, as you tramp away to another little rest-house in another station. Their voices will call after you: 'Father, come soon, come to us soon again, do not forget us!' You will not forget – but you cannot come *soon*. You cannot come again until you have done the whole circle of the bush-stations, night-stop by night-stop, rest-house by rest-house. And you know something of the compassion of Christ: 'He had compassion on the multitudes, because they were distressed and lying like sheep that have no shepherd. Then he said to his disciples: The harvest indeed is great, but the labourers are few ...'

Why not be a missionary?

As having nothing and possessing all things

(June/July 1960)

The car surges up the hill from the river with a roaring whine, gathers speed where the ground levels off, sings a high steady song as it grows small away down the forest road. Someone in a hurry. Someone keeping the horn going in short blasts to warn the weaving cyclists to the sides. And that someone could be you, John Smith. That could be you, eight or nine years from now, speeding through a palm forest in Africa about a missionary's business. Heading for an out-station, hurrying on a sick call, going to a meeting – or even joyriding (for, let's be straight, missionaries do that too on the rare occasions when they have time and chance!). It could be you, driving consciously, enjoying your skill, as a good driver sometimes does. Or it could be you driving automatically, your mind on the emergency of the moment, your stomach sick at the recollection of mangled bodies in a lorry accident back at the bridge, all your will fixed on getting to hospital in time with the little boy who is bleeding to death on the back seat.

Yes, it *could* be you, but don't get us wrong about the car. We're not holding *that* out as a bait. We shouldn't be *honest* if we did. It's this way: some missions will have a car, others won't. Suppose you're in one that has, here's what's likely to happen. You'll get back from a job some evening just around dark, after the mail-runner has made his round. There will be a letter for you. The substance of it will be that your bishop thinks the world of you and is well aware that you've been doing wonderfully in this station. He hates to have to do it, but he must now ask you to drop everything and transfer forthwith to the mission at XYZ. Well, you'll know – XYZ hasn't a car. XYZ hasn't a road or a bridge. XYZ is in the deep, deep bush, and all your getting around will have to be done on the two feet God gave you.

You're not superhuman. You won't *enjoy* separation from conveniences to which you have become accustomed. But what of it! A car is not all that important. A transfer, though, involves more than that. It means leaving people you're fond of, forsaking a football team or a choir that you've been building up, dropping some great project on which you're engaged – like a new church half-way built, or a group of booming out-stations that you've nursed along from nothing. A transfer means pulling yourself up by the roots. And that hurts – sometimes it hurts a lot.

When you make the initial sacrifice of a missionary and leave family, friends and possessions – don't imagine that's the end of giving. In the nature of things, you will make new friends in new places, set up a new home of sorts. You'll be called upon to leave these too, maybe over and over again. You're recalled from the missions to fill a post on the home front. You pull up the roots and come. By the time your term of office has run, you're dug in again. And again you must go. St Paul summed it up when he said of apostles in general that they had *no fixed abode*. God asks you for a sacrifice at the beginning – but he keeps on asking, and there's always something more to give him.

You let yourself in for this when you become a missionary – and how is *that* for bait? One day the apostles woke up to the fact that they had delivered themselves over completely to Christ, and they were startled at what that implied. Peter spoke for them all: 'Behold, we have left *all* and followed thee: what then shall we have?' They needn't have worried. Christ knew better than they how complete was their sacrifice, and how lifelong must be their unselfishness. He had the answer ready. If you *care* to read it (Mt 19:27-30) you won't have any doubt that the sacrifice makes sense.

Why not be a missionary?

Look upon us

(October 1961)

They carried him that morning as usual to the gate of the temple that is called Beautiful, and they laid him down there in the path of the people who, all day long, would be passing up to say their prayers. He made his little speech over and over again, and sometimes a passer-by tossed him alms, but mostly the people walked past as if he were not there. Then, at the ninth hour there came two men who looked at him with a strange intensity and he made the little speech again – crippled from birth, unable to help himself, unable to earn a living like other men – alms, kind sirs, in the name of God!

The bigger of the men said a curious thing. He said: '*Look upon us.*' Well, he looked 'earnestly' upon them, 'hoping that he should receive something of them'. Not indeed that there *was* much hope. His experienced eye sized them up for what they were, two country cousins without much spending money. Weathered features, sun-bleached hair, hard, clean hands – fishermen, probably. Galileans, by their accent. Some prospect! And here it was now – the brush-off! 'Silver and gold I have none ...' So now they'd probably promise to pray for him! He knew the line!

The thought died stillborn. The big man was still speaking. 'Silver and gold I have none, but what I have I give thee. In the name of Jesus Christ of Nazareth, arise and walk!' Peter's right hand grasping his. Peter helping him to his feet; strength flowing into 'his feet and soles'. Suddenly he could walk – and leap. The lame man went up with Peter and John into the temple, 'walking and leaping and praising God'. Then the crowd was running together to see the wonder and Peter was preaching like a man inspired, 'and the number of converts was five thousand'. A grand story from the Acts, one worth reading.

Look upon us. The pagan of the 1960s looks upon the missionary. What does he see? Not another scheming European hoping to use him for commercial gain or political leverage. This sweating, patient, dust-grimed man is not in league with the powerful, and patently, he is not numbered among the rich. Not a hopeful prospect for a *touch* then, though it is a fact well-known that he and his kind are healing the sick and feeding the needy and teaching the ignorant. This man offers nothing but a creed and a name. The creed is a creed of sacrifice and self-denial – but it rings true. The name is of one who was despised and ignominiously done to death, but the name speaks to the heart. For this creed and in this name the missionary will go, unprotesting, into captivity; he will go even to death.

He is a fool then – perhaps; or *is* he? Surely he is not powerful, but men trust him, thousands follow him. That is undeniable. He has no silver or gold, but he gives away freely what silver and gold cannot buy, things like peace, happiness, comfort, hope, compassion. He is a nobody, yet he speaks with confidence and authority and men listen and are convinced. He is a foreigner, yet he is closer to a man than his own brother. He pleads what, on the face of it, looks like a poor case, but he will not take no for an answer.

Why not be a missionary?

A street called Strait

(March 1962)

If you'd felt that Saul of Tarsus was a dangerous busybody, you'd have had the opinion of a good many honest Christians to back you. If you'd called him over-zealous, cocksure, even maybe sanctimonious, you mightn't have been too far from the truth. If you'd watched him approaching Damascus like a conquering hero, very sure of himself, with his letters of authority in his pocket, and said to yourself: the man is riding for a fall – you'd have been dead right. Two things, though, you couldn't have denied. One: Saul of Tarsus was a good man. Two: Saul of Tarsus wanted, very much, to do God's will.

The trouble was, though, that he had the wrong notion about God's will. He thought that God wanted him to destroy the Christians. What God actually wanted was to make the whole world Christian ... and Saul of Tarsus, though he didn't know it yet, was God's *vessel of election* to carry the Christian gospel to the ends of the earth. *God wanted Saul of Tarsus to be a missionary.* And right there on the road leading into Damascus, Saul got what many a young man after him was to get ... a bit of *vocation trouble!*

He found himself struck to the ground, blinded by a great light, rebuked by the voice of Christ. Suddenly, the cocksure Saul wasn't sure of anything any more. Instead he was frightened, bewildered, and in doubt. Now, let's see what steps Saul took to resolve his doubt.

First of all, he *prayed for guidance: 'Lord, what wilt thou have me to do?'* Right away, he was given sufficient guidance for his immediate needs; he was told to go on into the city and hold himself in readiness for further instructions. Meanwhile, these further instructions were being made known, in a vision, to a man named Ananias. God was, *in his own way,* looking after Saul.

Now, God's way of making his will known to Saul is a little surprising. God doesn't tell him directly. He makes him *wait* a little, perhaps in order that he may prepare himself by further prayer. (Saul does exactly this, as a matter of fact – Ananias is told that the Tarsus man he is to seek out in a street called Strait *is at his prayers.*) And here's a thing to note: when God does eventually make his will known to Saul, he does so *through the instrumentality of Ananias*. In other words, Saul has to take guidance not from God directly but from another man like himself. It is Ananias who restores his sight and tells him what he is to do.

So now we have, straight out of the Acts of the Apostles (chapter nine), a lesson to guide John Smith when he gets *vocation trouble*. Four things: readiness to do God's will; prayer for guidance; patience – no hurry, no panic, just confident waiting for God's will to become clear; and, finally, willingness to accept counsel from someone who is qualified to give it.

It's this fourth lesson that John Smith usually baulks at! John Smith likes to stand on his own feet. He doesn't like being dependent on other people. He doesn't like *opening up*, even to a priest, even when so important a thing as his life's vocation is in question. Well, Saul probably didn't like having to be led into the city by the hand – but he couldn't see, so it was the only way. And whether he liked taking his instructions from Ananias or not, that was the way God wanted him to get them. And you won't forget, will you, John Smith, that Saul, otherwise Paul, turned out to be something extra special in the way of a missionary!

Why not be a missionary?

A clean desk

(March 1963)

Fifty miles north is the international frontier. Forty miles south is a town and port. From the town to the frontier – that's the parish. Eastwards, twenty miles or so, again a frontier. Westwards – fifteen, twenty miles – is the river. It's all yours, between the frontier and the river. A lot of square miles; forest, jungle, little mountains – and a winding ribbon of road from north to south with jungle paths branching off it here and there to the villages. You drive the road north and south, in a six-year-old Volkswagen. You walk the paths, five hours, six hours – under the gloom of the forest, you don't think in hours, really; you just march along till you reach somewhere. You know that wherever there's a path, there's a village at the end of it. The village is your business. All the forest villages. All the camps in the rubber plantations and the oil plantations. All the scattered homesteads of the settlers in the Land Development Scheme. Perhaps eight thousand people, and more coming in all the time. All your business.

It's not so much that the people are so many; but that one parish priest has so much ground to cover. Even the people see the humour of it. They see you haring up or down the road in the old Volkswagen, slithering around the hairpin bends, bogging in the mud, skidding in the dust, or tramping along the little paths to the villages; trying to keep the whole place covered. And sometimes they tell you jokingly that you are like a landlord all the time travelling on his estate.

They call you *the Father* – always using the definite article as though you were the only priest in the world. You're the only one *they* see, months and months on end. But they know, at least, that *you* are always there, and always at their service. They'll come to your small house, halfway up the road, when they want to see you. If you're not there, they know you'll be coming back, so they'll sit down and wait. You'll turn up that night, or the next night, for sure. You'll be there at your desk in the parish office certainly within twenty-four hours at the outside, open to all comers.

Maybe they don't know *why* you come back so regularly to

that desk, or why you're so scrupulously careful to keep the *in* basket cleared and the *pending* basket under observation. Maybe they cannot imagine why you're so fussy about keeping a clean desk and up-to-the-minute files. But that's the way it's got to be in a big one-man mission. You can't possibly hope to cover all the ground alone, or to reach all the work. So you organise helpers all over the parish who will keep the wheels turning even when you are not with them. And you work from one centre where you can always be reached, and try to run the organisation you've built up at peak efficiency.

That means a lot of writing, a good many laborious hours at the desk, a great deal of planning and follow-through. But it pays off. And come to think of it, St Paul had a lot of letters to write. And that was long ago; and he didn't have a typewriter or a filing system, or any of the handy mechanical gadgets that save you so much time and sweat!

Why not be a missionary?

Nobody is a nobody

(April 1964)

Maybe it's not big enough to be called a city. A couple of miles of waterfront, with tugs and ships and river-craft; a tight-packed huddle and sprawl of buildings up the hill faces, spilling over the plateau to the isolated farms at the edge of the forest; noises and smells and milling traffic; jazz music blaring endlessly from a thousand radios, people thronging, hurrying, shouting, laughing, quarrelling, through the streets and markets. Say, forty, fifty thousand people. Small city, big town, that's it.

It belongs to you. You belong to it. You are the parish priest. Nothing to it, much; just so long as you see to it that you're always – but *always* – available; and *equally* available to rich and poor, Christian, non-Christian, the lot. They've got to know that; you've got to make it clear. Once they know it, they'll trust you, and they'll forgive you most of your mistakes. And you'll make plenty. That won't matter, so long as you learn from them!

You've got to have *time* for everyone; and that's the crux; because there's never enough time. So you're fussy about punctuality, finicky about order; you keep on trying to streamline the organisation, to be an economist about time and motion. At least, that's the principle; but the practice has to be flexible, because there's a lot of disorder, unpunctuality, even unreasonableness, to be found in fifty thousand normal human beings.

Human beings – every one of them, and *each* one entitled individually to your respect, your time, your sweat. Important meeting with the city fathers on matters of high policy; but you've got to walk out on them because some down-and-out from the gutter sends word he's dying, and wants you. Social occasion with the town's élite; but you excuse yourself, because some insignificant family in a backstreet has a row it can't settle without getting you in as a mediator. Mornings, with a whole day's urgencies screaming for priority, you'll sit quietly listening while some little nobody stammers out the devastating worry he can no longer carry alone. When you're a pastor, nobody is *ever* a nobody – and the human distress of a garbage collector is mountains more important than the visit of a Head of State.

You're a public figure. Everyone knows you. You're hated, loved, praised, misrepresented, defended, calumniated. You're fair game even for the newspapers; they'll praise you for insufficient cause and blame you for the wrong reasons. You take it in your stride – you don't work for the newspapers.

You sweat in the January heats, and feel the depression of the August rains, and suffer the screaming tension of the tornado seasons. But all days are the same, with morning crowds at your door, a telephone ringing at your elbow, a pile of work on your desk, and people, always people wanting you. All the nights are the same, too; and you sleep with one eye open, one ear alert for the sick call bell that's *bound* to ring its panic note through the darkness. Well, that's the sort of life it is, when you divide yourself on fifty thousand people. Hard enough going, but there's nothing to it, much. And people sometimes *do* say thanks!

Why not be a missionary?

Walk tall

(April 1965)

I could show you the letter that makes all this legal and upright and even meritorious; but, *brother*, you change places with me this strange sad morning and, letter or no letter, you'll feel like a criminal. I'll never know how, but I got through the goodbyes with a bright face, making bright promises. They looked at me. What was it in their faces – resignation, reproach, love, understanding? I don't know. What I saw in their eyes – mostly dry – was *need*. I handed out reassurances. And then, at last, I drove away from it all, down the bush road to the tarmac highway, and I put the boot to the floor, and the old car rattled and sent up dust. Goodbye little mission. We had good days together. Now I must try not to think of you.

I speed past the end of a bush path, firmly not looking. Two critically sick people up that path need looking after. Who's going to look after them now? Who's going to take care of the sick ones, the troubled ones? What's to become of the old folk? – 'Father,' they always say, 'when the end is near, you will be with me, and it will be easy to die.' *Traitor*, says my mind. And the children? We had such plans. The weak ones that need constant chivvying? The two score really holy ones, climbing high, saints unawares? The Saturday evening hordes for confession? Forget it! Forget it! It can't be helped. A man dies up country. A man falls sick. Two gaps. No replacements. So you do the best you can for the *majority*. The ten thousand I'm leaving don't need *me*. They just need a priest – any priest. But ten times ten thousand need a priest at the end of this stretch of tarmac. A strong argument. Sweetly reasonable.

The letter in my pocket proves it's not my doing, not my choosing. But this morning I took the veil off the empty tabernacle. I turned the key in the door of my small house. That small house was always open; the tabernacle was never empty before. This morning I quenched the sanctuary lamp. I closed down a mission. The deed is done. Forget it. Take the long view. Walk tall.

My sick and troubled, my old folk, the children, the weak, the wild ones, the holy ones – I made them what promises I could. But I left them without a priest. I wonder what it feels like to be a

Christian without a priest! I promised them: Some day a priest will come. He will open up the little mission again. He'll put the pyx back in the tabernacle, replace the veil, light the lamp. Some day! But when? I don't know at all. As soon as there's a priest to spare. As soon as – John Smith, how would you like to light that lamp?

Why not be a missionary?

On the move

(August/September 1965)

You drove through the greening countryside and last week's cold was a memory almost obliterated by the delight of this first perfect spring day. You drove through a quiet land of Friesian herds and tilling tractors. The car ran sweetly, unhurried. The sun shone – the homeland was very dear. You said sentimental goodbyes to the familiar mountains as they slipped back one by one. You said thanks to God for the peace and plenty, for the greening countryside and the warming sun. You were leaving it. In your mind, you had already left it. The road you followed led on through the airport, into the south eastern sky, far and away …

Three glaring airports and twenty hours later, you came down out of the dull steaming dawn and said thanks to God again. Thanks to be back. Thanks for the customs man who said, 'God bless you', as he made his chalk-squiggle on your luggage. Thanks for the nameless boy who carried your things just as the unaccustomed heat and the wrong kind of clothing made the sweat start out on you. Thanks for the considerate confrère who got up early to come the miles out of town to meet you. And thanks for the crazy traffic, the jostling noisy crowds, the sights and the sounds and the smells that suddenly bridged the years for you and filled you all over again with the wonder of your first assay into Africa.

It was so long ago, and Africa and you had come such a long, long way since that first meeting to this latest. The new emancipated Africa, whirling in a purposeful confusion, trying to do ten thousand things at once. And the new you, still adaptable enough, thank heavens, to adjust to the reeling pace and the prospect of ten thousand things of your own that must be attended to. So, you start again, and somehow or other, you are picking up the threads, and fighting the traffic, and steeling your countrybred mind to the fantastic glare and noise and heat and confusion of a vast tropical city.

So many times over, through the years, you have packed your luggage – what there was of it – and stayed near a telephone waiting for the details of a new assignment. So many times you have said your goodbyes to the countryside, in the deep cold winter or the high summer, or, like this time, in the suddenly awakening spring ... immunised already to the parting by preoccupation with the unpredictables of the job ahead. So many parts of the world. So many cares and challenges. So many people, met as strangers, parted from as friends, with a pang in the heart ...

No roots, no fixed abode, no entanglements; jealously-guarded freedom to move or to stay as the situation indicates. It has to be that way when you're a specialist missionary, liable to a whole succession of specialist assignments in a whole lot of different places. Maybe it's lonely sometimes. Maybe you do wish for a quiet time somewhere in the future when you'll hang up your hat and find shelves for your books and tell yourself, 'I've come to stay.' But you know it's just a pipedream. Or, at any rate, you know that as long as your special expertise is of service to God or the people of God ... that long, you're going to stay on the move, airport to airport, continent to continent; crossing your own tracks in the pathless air across the world, over and over again. It will be time though to rest in one place when you have no more to give. Meanwhile, over and over again: 'Goodbye, I'll be back sometime, maybe,' and thank God for the mountains that soothe the heart at parting; thank God for the going, and thank God for the arriving, and thank him for the returning – when it comes.

Why not be a missionary?

Man in a jam

(November 1965)

You weave a careful path through throngs of jaywalkers. Two motor scooters pass on the inside, wobbling crazily through the potholes off the edge of the tar. The bus just ahead stops suddenly without signalling, and you're too close to pull out. A taxi roars out past you with the horn blaring. Two other taxis and a private car follow him. They meet a down-coming lorry before they can find a space to pull back into the line – and that's that. Everything grinds to a halt in insoluble deadlock. The street jams solid. So here's where we settle down for a long, long wait. No use getting mad. No use at all to lean on the horn-button. Nothing can move – except the pedestrians. Now they swarm uninhibited through the stalled traffic. Now the cheerful gibes go back and forth ... and now, out of the nameless, faceless throng, comes an individual ...

He gives you a smile as he approaches, half sympathy, half mockery. You shrug expressively and give him a smile back. Then he's leaning two elbows on the window-sill, and the smile is gone. Without preamble, out of the soundless depths of one man's loneliness of spirit, there pours into your ears a tale of such anguished defeat and desolation that you are moved almost to tears. Now you are no longer a tired commuter fighting his way home from work through the heat and smell of traffic. Now the vast impatiences of the road dwindle into insignificance. Now you are the priest, alone with one soul out of the thousands.

Call it a very simple theology, or call it a very complicated providence, but to you it seems like this: God stopped the traffic and this one man in grave need saw you in your white cassock sitting sweating at the wheel of a light-blue Volkswagen. This one man grasped at a fleeting grace. He took advantage of a traffic-jam to unburden his overwrought spirit and seek comfort. Years back, away down in the bush country, he had known a priest who was kind. In his mind, therefore, all priests were kind. Therefore, this stranger priest, caught in the traffic of the inhuman city, would listen to him and help him. This one would speak comfort to him, and be his friend. He would even use this immobilised car in this milling street as a confessional, on request. He would, further, make appointments to rectify a marriage and baptise children and conduct peace talks with in-laws. He would stave off an eviction, go security for a small loan, and use his contacts to find an unemployed man a job …

And that's the way it was – for one individual who came unbidden out of a faceless crowd and took shape as a person. That's the way it was, this time – and many times. God stopped the traffic to give grace …

But this time, like every other time, when the traffic moved again and you drove on, you were left with the despairing question: 'But what happens *to the others?*' Who cares for the thronging thousands on this street and every other street? Who will bring priests to all these, to listen to their woes with kindness and heal their wounded spirit with sympathy and sacrament? Ten priests to a million people! 'What are these among so many!'

Why not be a missionary?

Scraping the barrel

(October 1966)

Everything is ready. The tables are laid. The great feast is waiting for the guests. Only thing is – there *are* no guests. So the host paces the floor, hurt and disappointed, and the servants come in with the thin excuses from the unwilling folk who have got the invitations. 'I bought a farm ... I married a wife ... I'm trying out a new team of oxen ... Can't come ... Sorry.'

The host is indignant, insulted, let down. 'I have prepared a feast,' he says, 'and it is going to be eaten. If these people won't come I'll find others who will. Go out into the streets and homes. Go out into the highways and hedges – bring in anyone you meet.'

John Smith, friend, isn't it a terrible thought that the good Lord maybe has to scrape the bottom of the barrel to find men willing to be priests?

There's no doubt that he could find many a one more brainy, more persuasive, more all-round-better-suited for the priesthood than some of the people who actually end up priests. So why doesn't he pick them? Maybe the answer is that they won't let themselves be picked! And if they won't let themselves be picked, that's curtains as far as they are concerned; because if a man chooses the priesthood, he's got to choose it freely.

So the Lord has to scrape the barrel – and he comes up with John Smith! Okay, maybe John Smith is not the best suited, or the brainiest, or the most persuasive – but the difference between him and the others is that he looks the Lord in the face and then he looks into his own heart – and whatever misgivings he has, he finds he can't make the thin excuse. He can't find it in himself to say *no* to Jesus Christ.

So he says *yes* – Lord, if you want it that way, you must know you're not getting much of a bargain, but if it's okay with you, it's okay with me. I'll do the best I can. You just pile on the help.

Not all the top-rankers say *no*, mind you, but if you read a bit of history you'll likely reach the conclusion that it was largely the five-eighth blokes like yourself that kept the show going for the past two thousand years.

Why not be a missionary?

Crazy, man!

(January/February 1967)

Know something? You've missed a deadline. An editor with a gripe is biting his nails and scowling at you across four thousand miles of land and sea. If you don't sit right down and rap out the monthly stint, if you don't get it on tomorrow's plane, his publishing schedule is going to be knocked cockeyed, the printer is going to be breathing down his neck, and his distribution arrangements are going to be in chaos. Everybody is going to love you!

You're making me cry. Look, it's rained and rained and rained for two days without any let-up. Then today you could hardly lift your hand because the heat and the humidity had you knocked flat. And it was Sunday ... and does anybody have any idea what three crowded public Masses in a row in ninety-degree heat with thousands of communions ... does anybody have any idea what that kind of a morning can do to a man? Plus meetings that went on and on. Plus a few awkward sick calls. Plus evening devotions. Plus knowing that there must be what passes for a fresh breeze in these parts down at the sea – if you could make time to get down to the sea. (What hope!) Has anyone got any idea how demanding a parish full of people can be – every single one thinking that he's the only man on the island and that you've got all the time in the world to give him. And every single one talking round and round the thing he came to see you about, but never coming to the point. So that you want to scream. Want to smash something. Give short answers, blow your top, forget that this ... all this ... is your job. People are your job. Unreasonable, awkward, exasperating, whining, utterly dependent people. Clinging to you as if you'd been made of steel and concrete: as if you'd been specially designed to carry the world on your back ... as if you'd been equipped with vertebrae and everyone else had been born without any ...

And then ... this. Sit down near midnight with the sweat streaming and knock out seven hundred words for the editor. Ladies and gentlemen, observe my sleeves; there's nothing up them. I will not produce ... *presto!* ... seven hundred words of searing exhortation out of my sun-helmet for a hypothetical reader ... who, if I can lure him away from his heavy metal sound long enough to read them, may perhaps then decide to exchange all *that* for all *this*. He'll need to be *crazy* ... but then he probably is.

At least I hope he is. Crazy enough to want to do what I've been doing for so many years. Days like this – not all so heavy, sure, but plenty of them like today. People like this ... demanding, unreasonable, dependent ... You tell yourself that you can't stand them any more, but then trouble or danger threaten them and you want to put your arms around them all together and keep them from harm.

You can't do it forever though. Someone's got to follow on. So you sit down and sweat out those seven hundred words to the editor at the end of a long day. Maybe they'll go over his head. Maybe he won't even read them. You'll never know, one way or the other. But this is another part of this impossible day ... and now thank heavens it's done for another month ... and ladies and gentlemen, I have to be up at a quarter to six. I'm going to bed. Hold it ... oh no ... not another sick call ... oh well!

Why not be a missionary?

Hating the children

(May 1968)

It was the Mass of an abbot, and Peter asked his quarrelsome question as usual in the gospel: '*We* have left all things – what therefore shall we have?'; and when I got to the bit about the son of man sitting on the throne of his glory, there was a bit of subdued sobbing out front and I said to myself, 'Mm-mmh! what's this?' Lay missionary Kathy told me afterwards with a grin: 'I said to the Lord – I don't want to sit on any of those twelve thrones – I'm so darned tired that I want to lie down and sleep for all eternity …'

We'd been having it rough for months and we were all just about played out, with a major or mini crisis every day and the work piling on us and no relief or reinforcement in sight – and nearly all of us overdue for leave. We're not a very emotional team, but all of us admitted that odd things were now and then making us *weepy*.

Like the evening I went looking for someone in a mission nearby, and I picked up *Ireland of the Welcomes* while I was waiting for my man, and it opened at a picture of a glorious summer beach I used to know very well and – well, I just dropped the book and switched quickly to something else.

It was the same day that I'd received a joyous letter from a well-loved niece telling me she was going to be a mother, and I'd been foolishly dwelling on all the bits I'd missed out of her life. I hadn't been anywhere near when she was married, and I'd missed the years from fourteen to seventeen, and before that the years from seven to twelve, and the same thing was happening now with a dozen of her brothers, sisters and cousins. There were the odd glorious months every few years when we were all together and shared mountains and concerts, dreams and rebellions, and drew the bonds of shared blood tight all over again … with always the rasping separation at the end …

Once upon a time, I'd have been affected like Kathy by the gospel of an abbot. Not any longer. Let the reward at the end take care of itself. But for now I need the grim reassurance of the martyr-bishop gospel: 'If any man come to me, hating not his father and mother, brothers, sisters, wife, lands – yes, and his own life also, he cannot be my disciple …'

HATING THE CHILDREN

The mother and father problem is solved for me – let's not twist the knife in that old wound. And the brothers and sisters – I can by now accept the casual comings and goings matter-of-factly enough.

But the children, Lord – I wonder why you didn't mention the children? With them, I've got to learn to *hate* all over again, and there's one thing sure – your *disciples* don't ever get a chance to let their sacrifice go stale!

Why not be a missionary?

Checking the price tag

(June/July 1968)

He was a fine specimen, vigorous and forthright, and straight as a die. Not much with twenty; only a boy really. But you knew from the way he looked at you, straight in the eye without fear or insolence, that there were no deep troubles or complexes; there was little in his life of which he might be ashamed. He was the sort of boy any father or mother would be proud of. The sort of boy who would have made a fine priest. The sort that Christ was looking for.

They faced each other, Christ and this youth. And Christ made his proposition. 'Go sell what you have and give to the poor ... and come follow me.' We call it a *vocation* nowadays and the price, from the beginning, was the same – everything you have. The young man might have thought up a few really good excuses, played a bit for time. But he didn't. He wasn't the type. He knew for certain that the cost was too great. Giving up all meant giving up too much. And he knew in his quick, incisive way that there just couldn't be any bargaining, any meeting half-way. He would have loved to have followed, he felt the magnetism, but ... wordlessly, he turned away, sad. Jesus Christ looked after him as he went. He had been turned down flat.

'Because he had great possessions.' Maybe a big family business in Jerusalem or vineyards in Judea or wheatlands in Galilee or even a camel train plying to Damascus and places east. What would he have done if he could have given up these things? Become a great apostle? Carried the faith across the Sahara or to fabled Cathay? Nobody knows. We only know that Christ invited him specially, obviously wanted what only he could give. And that he was refused. We know, too, that millions south of the Sahara are still waiting while Cathay is more inaccessible now than it was two thousand years ago. And there isn't even a rock or a tree stump or a rood of ground in the Holy Land today that the guides can point to and say: 'This was part of the wealth of the rich young man.' Not a trace remains.

Yes, it was a pity. He shouldn't have turned away. It is so easy to make rules for other people and make excuses for one-self. If Christ is offering you his priesthood, John Smith, the price tag is still big. A great profession or a well-paid job or wide green acres that your grandfather called home. Everything you have or will ever become. And you know what you're buying: hard work, opposition, dislike and contempt maybe, because the servant can't expect more than his master. That and a mysterious, intimate fellowship adds a new dimension to love.

The choice is free and all yours, John Smith. You know what another young man did. What of you?

Why not be a missionary?

Other cities

(December 1969)

Lather up and rasp away. One thing, anyway, shaving's easy here. Water always warm, or warmish. No mirror, just a testing fingertip. Enjoy the view. Bougainvillaea bloom looping, rioting along the verandah poles. Frangipani, jacaranda, flame blossom, mangos in fruit. The tawny endless plain under the sky with the great cattle herds moving. And the little dawn breeze whispering, fragrant from the dry infinities.

Crown-birds calling, guinea-fowl, parrots piping high up in flight, cardinal birds, canaries, budgerigars. Baboons coughing to one another down there in the copse of the river. Milkmaids swinging along to market. Calabashes on their heads. Silver bangles above the elbows. Necklaces of moonstones big as bantam's eggs. Leather-hatted herdsmen with staves. The odd donkey. And a camel or two.

Oh God, it's happy and beautiful, and wherever I go I will never forget these mornings between the rains and the harmattan. Nor the villages, nor the children, nor the white flour bursting out of the guinea-corn between the millstones, nor the groundnut pyramids nor the brown walls of the towns with their parapets, nor the whorls of the painted signs on the houses, nor the white robes of men yarning under the shade-trees. The red roads. The clenched fist salutes. The gentleness of a child's hand leading me by one finger into the welcome of her mother's compound in the tall grass. These things I will not forget.

But I will leave them behind. Soon, and once and for all and – but who knows? – for ever. For I must go. I must get up and go. To other cities I must preach. Other cities, other peoples. Come over to us. Walk among us. Come on over. Patrick and Paul – and Christ – would understand. They knew the hunger. Heard those voices. Swallowed down the heartbreak and struck the road.

Me, too. Three thousand days here on the knoll above the savannah. Built the house, planted the mangos, gathered a people, taught them, poured water, broke the bread, healed with anointing, imposed hands when the words were spoken that commissioned my successor, stood by him till he was ready to carry on alone. And that's now. Time to set out. Start again. Other cities ...

You think it comes natural? Stay three thousand days, but on your life put down no roots? You think I took it on because it was easy? You think I didn't know? Oh, I knew, or – but no, honestly, you *can't* know, not till the job is done and you take your hat off the peg. Then you know. It hurts and it costs. But it's better than the restlessness. Better than the uneasiness, the discontent, when you've stayed a day too long and you remember what you are and you lift up your eyes and see the harvest, out there, waiting.

Why not be a missionary?

Knife twist

(January/February 1970)

One village or
a hundred, with a welcome
for certain if I came.
The headmen and I
would double-clasp each other's hands
and feel the years
of friendship
through the fingers; there would
be laughter and children's shouts,
glad drums under the moon;
they'd rig some sort of
confessional in a cool place
and I'd go to work,
like the old days.
Latecomers in the morning
Mass
Communions
Till the arms ached,
and sweat
Stinging the eyes.
A road here reminds me
of a road there;
a voice, a tune, a colour,
a smell, a feeling, a change in
the weather
brings it all back;
I stand still, suddenly, not
breathing, five full seconds while
the knife twists; and
a prayer escapes out of the
pain and happiness of
remembering
for Dominic, Bruno, Raphael, John,
Paulina, Bernard, and
the children; but
they've grown up now, of course;

and would hardly remember me.
I could find the paths in my sleep, and
no pausing to wonder indecisive
at intersections.
I know just how the first
house will look,
cornerwise to the brown street
fresh-thatched for the rains,
and the oil-press working
in the scatter of palm-kernels.
When I go back some day
I know how it will be –
But I'm not fooling
myself or anyone;
there's not a chance I'll go;
life is not long enough
for sentimental journeys,
or moping, or nostalgia.
No, all that
was the old days; it was *then;*
Here and now
the plans, projects, people, snags,
responsibilities, the other
cities, villages, jobs, that
come with the seventies;
start something, sweat at it,
hand it over as a
going concern; move, launch
out again; whip the fading
energy to the new task; move quickly
again when the word comes.
When I have time to go back,
I'll be too old to travel,
or too dead! We'll wait to
play the drums, clasp the hands;
There will be time, on
resurrection day.

        Why not be a missionary?

Value for time

(April 1971)

I always liked pop. More or less grew up on Elvis – and of course rock. I can even remember Sinatra. Spent my share on *singles* and collected the centre spreads and even joined a fan club or two. And I haven't exactly switched off entirely, even now. The little transistor isn't the greatest and my listening is – well, somewhat erratic. But I still have a fair idea of what's heading for the top of the charts. It gives one a contact point with young people here, too. So I can claim to have *pastoral reasons* for tuning in, if I start feeling guilty.

What got me out here in the first place? How did I decide to opt for the life (besides God's grace, that is)? Well, we used to do a lot of thinking, behind all the noise and carry-on. Even the crazy ones you'd never suspect. Deep water under all the froth, I suppose. Not any sort of organised, cerebral action; just maybe lazing in bed, or lying on one's back on a hot day, or (officially) studying a textbook on a wet winter evening. Thinking about life, about what was happening, about the future.

There wasn't any TV then – when I was in secondary school – but I did read a lot. Newspapers, as well as thrillers and the occasional *better book*. Rip Kirby got me started on newspapers early on. I began to notice things. Like the way names made headlines, stayed around for a while, even a few years maybe, and then they were gone. Nobody remembered them any more. As if they were never born. Others, new names, crowded in to fill their places. Newspapers, TV, radio – the media as we call them nowadays – always abhorred a vacuum. Nothing was for ever. Or, was there ... something?

One wanted to make a mark, to contribute. And one had only so long; every day counted. I could have gone for money and the Mercedes bit; I might have made it or I might not. One thing was sure – that would pass too, like the spot in the headlines. You just couldn't take it with you. So I figured there had to be something else. Something that made sense in the long term. So I made my decision.

You see it *is* possible to make a mark nobody is going to wipe out, to start something that will survive. To get value for your time. Something you can take with you, even after the final curtain. But it needs plenty of hard thinking to get it straight. Praying a little about it helps more than a little. And another thing ... like all things worthwhile, it can be tough going ... but it can be fun too.

Why not be a missionary?

The rights and wrongs of it

(October 1972)

Once upon a time – and pardon me for mentioning it – the Son of God said to us: 'Ask and you shall receive.' Simple and straight like that. No complications or conditions or ifs or buts. No double talk. And once upon a time a lot of us believed him.

A lot of us still do. But you'd never think it! Not when you listen to the groaning we go on with. Or feel the chill of our gloom and pessimism about one certain subject. Namely, the future of the Catholic priesthood.

The boom is over, we say. *Vocations* are finished. Might as well face it and sell off the seminaries to the hotel companies. (Tourism will probably pick up – no trouble being optimistic about important things like money.)

And let's dishearten ourselves properly while we're about it – the vocations boom was probably *artificial* anyway; times were bad and the priesthood offered security. It was all an economic thing.

Walk softly, friends, you're treading on my dreams. I thought I became a priest for better reasons. It was bread and butter all the time, you say! Well, what do you know!

And all the priests and missionaries of our time were fooling themselves, too? You know, that must have happened unknown to God. And the young Christian nations are just the chance outcome of economic hardship in Belgium, France, Holland, Ireland, the United States and Canada? It must be a bit of a surprise to God to see how full their seminaries are today, mustn't it?

Maybe the difference between the young Christian nations and us is that they take Christ at his word. They're not afraid their prayers won't be answered. No, and they're not afraid they *will* be answered, either. Which latter just might be our trouble!

Ask and you shall receive. 'Too easily,' someone wrote recently, 'we interpret this word of Our Lord as a promise. It is also a threat.' Ask for priestly vocations in the family and – you might get them; is that why we're not asking any more?

So there's a *vocations crisis* in the Church – your Church. Not so many willing to take on the priesthood now. Not so many ready to stay with it for a lifetime. The priesthood has always cost a lot, and the cost is higher than ever now.

So turn your back, John Smith. Pretend you don't see what your family is doing to your Church and to you. Bolster the fiction with comfortable sociological explanations of the vocations decline. Go along with them when they pray together for those honours in your Leaving Certficate for your university scholarship. When you're safely fixed in your profitable career, then you can take care of the rest of mankind – once you've paid off the mortgage and fixed things with the hire purchase and put the kids through school. What harm if the fire is gone out of you by then – what's wrong with a good Christian layman? The answer, of course, must be – nothing.

But you did say *Christian?* If the priesthood is in crisis or in danger of extinction, then certain things you stand for are under the gravest kind of threat. Let the priest disappear and goodbye to the Mass, the sacraments, the greater part of the machinery of grace. A good way to snuff out the decencies, the principles, and most of the things that make man better than an animal and the world better than a zoo.

Well, it's not going to happen. First of all, because Christ guaranteed – another guarantee – that the gates of hell would not prevail. And secondly, because certain people intend to see to it, by their personal intervention and personal commitment, that the priesthood remains and that the faith is handed on. There aren't any medals going for it at the moment, but they are very determined about this. And absolutely certain about what they're doing.

You don't have to do a thing about it, John Smith, but I think you won't want to be left out when there's a last ditch stand to be taken. If you're afraid you'll receive when you ask – well, you won't be the first.

Why not be a missionary?

Today is full of things I want to do

(November 1972)

Wake in the cool dawn. Bright and fair with traffic noise. One question answered – where am I? Now the reflex action of a morning offering of sorts. Thanks for the night. The day – all of it, Lord – is for you. Make it formal later, washed and conscious. Meanwhile, other essentials to establish, like – who am I, and what's the programme?

And today, like yesterday, like a lot of yesterdays, I am a priest. I don't know why. That is, I know why I became a priest, but I don't know why God let me. Probably because he could be certain nobody was ever going to think there was something special about me that made me a natural for the job. Always be entirely obvious, he could have done better for himself.

So forget about me. But don't underrate the priest bit. And don't think I do. I wasn't special before. I am now. And that goes for today and for every day to come. Because nothing's going to change about it. I was young when it happened. But not that young. Old enough to look this thing in the face and see what it demanded – the whole thing – and say: I'm taking this on now and I'm not going back on it. Ever. This is for life and beyond. And it's enough for me. More than enough.

And so ... goose pimples in the morning. Because the programme today, like yesterday, is the programme of a priest. The programme is to try to be holy. A little bit more every day. Does it make you laugh? Well, it makes me laugh too. I'm dead serious about it all the same. And wouldn't you be? It means today, every day, to be faithful, to be loyal, to gain that extra inch. Or anyway, to be on your feet, trying. That's what you took on, but one thing you learn, there's more to it than you thought. Which doesn't change anything. You take it in small bits, not all together. Every morning you say *yes* again ...

Is it worth it? Only one life to live and all the wonderful things a man could do ...

Well look! A big modern hospital you read about – they had to stop disposing of aborted babies in the incinerator in the basement. There was a law saying this had to be done in the public crematorium. No law against causing the abortions ... Three young men mow down passengers just off the plane ... A glossy pornographic magazine has a circulation of sixteen million ... White stomps on black ... Dedicated young men and women plant bombs in crowded department stores. Bang! So young people's legs get blown off and that proves something, maybe ... So you read your list of *causes* – things you feel mad about – hunger, injustice, oppression ... And what do you do about it? After protesting?

This is what I do. I know it's God's world. It needs a lot of goodness and grace to balance that horror. I aim to provide some. It needs pardon. I aim to earn it. It needs truth, I aim to tell the truth. You talk about civil rights, basic human rights. Liberty of expression. Free flow of information. Man has a right to know. So what are you going to do about telling him? The truth – all of it. The one thing that can make him free. You're right, it's my job. Thank you for a wonderful compliment.

You know, I don't in the least feel like a knight buckling on a shining armour. I just feel sleepy and I hate getting out of bed. So all right, maybe tonight when I answer the question – where am I, I'll find I'm still back there in square one. But today is full of things I want to do, and whatever I'm missing by being a priest, I wouldn't trade one of these things for it. I'll make some sort of stand for the decencies and for principles I believe in and I'll tell men the truth they have a right to know. I'll use the easy powers the priesthood has given me to give the world goodness and grace. I'll pay the cost, willingly. I'll keep on doing all that for a lifetime. Would you want any other kind of life? I don't.

Why not be a missionary?

Nobody you'd know

(May 1973)

Her name was Mary and she was – nobody. Nobody you'd have been likely to know. Unless it happened you were a friend of her son; then you'd have met her here and there. You might have been invited to family functions with him – maybe to the wedding of a relative – because she'd have known it would please him to have you along. You'd have been pleased too – not because of the food or the wine, but because she thought that much about you. You'd have been surprised how much her good opinion meant to you.

She was nobody out of the ordinary, you'd have thought; well, maybe, in a way ... but certainly nobody important. And still, when God's time came to fulfil the promise of the ages, it was to her his messenger came. She was everything God wanted the mother of his son to be. The choice was his, to make her exactly to his liking. You'd have found her without flaw.

She did have to say *yes*. God had made her human, and that meant he'd made her free. But once she agreed to what God proposed, the world could never be the same again. The terror of the night was finished. The noonday scourge need frighten us no more. The light that died in Eden could blaze again.

She came from the back of beyond. A village in the hills you'd have made jokes about. You'd never have thought of looking for the world's saviour there. But that's where he was, and that's where he stayed through his growing years. In the home she made for him, advancing in wisdom and age and grace.

She got no special notice before the public when the whole world went out after her son. She lost him once to his father's business; lost him next to the special group around him; lost him to the multitudes – to every cripple and beggar and ne'er-do-well, every crook, every misfortunate body with a pain, every soul with a sin, every devil-ridden misfit, every guilt-tortured derelict. She lost him finally to the scoffers, the spitters, the torturers, to the one who swung the weighted whiplash, to the man that drove the nails.

All the time he knew and she knew how much she counted.

That had to be enough. At the very end he let it be seen before the world how greatly she mattered to him ... to us.

So they rallied to her in the first uncertain days after he was taken up from them, and drew courage. She was there when the Spirit came and drove them out into the streets, when they spoke with fearless eloquence and men thought them drunk. She knew that nothing now could keep their feet off the roads of the world. And that they'd come back to her, always come back to her.

There is nothing more we know. Except, of course, that she in her turn was taken up, and that she is with God, and that she is ours, and that she waits for us. That it will please him to have us along, and so she must see we come.

Nobody you'd know? Well, it could have been like that. We're just the lucky ones. She'd expect us to bring home the others. Her son would be pleased to have them along. The rooms are ready and the feast is laid.

Why not be a missionary?

Stop fooling yourself

(June/July 1973)

When John the Baptist looked up from his work at the Jordan and saw the Pharisees coming, the first thing he did was call them a nasty name. Snakes, he called them. So right away they knew what he thought about them. He thought they were poison!

And he wasn't so far out, either. Still, he was willing to give them the benefit of the doubt. 'Maybe you do want to turn over a new leaf,' he said to them. 'Well, let's see you prove it. Suppose now you just cut out all the pious posing; start showing a little genuine charity, a small bit of real compassion; stop behaving as if everyone else was dirt. Then maybe God will believe you!'

The impudence of the man took their breath away. But he had more surprises for them. He rubbed it in well. 'It's not going to do you any good telling yourselves: We are God's chosen ones, we are the children of Abraham. Maybe you won't believe it, but if God wants to he can take the stones here and turn *them* into children of Abraham. No trouble to him.'

Well, after that, it was a safe bet that John wouldn't win any popularity contests among the Pharisees. It was pretty bad to call them poisonous vipers, but to suggest that God might pick rank outsiders to be his chosen people – this they couldn't stomach, this was intolerable. Because it would put them on the outside.

From there on, they had the hatchets out. They were gunning for John the Baptist.

And it wasn't too long before they were gunning for Christ. Because Christ turned out to have the same sort of liberal ideas as John. Christ wanted everyone in. Oh, and he wanted justice for all. He wanted every man respected. He told dangerous stories about publicans going down justified from the temple while Pharisees prayed in vain. Well, they'd get him!

So they asked him innocent questions – is it lawful to pay taxes to Caesar? And he stood there with the penny in his hand and just looked at them. *Why do you set traps for me?* And gave them an answer that defeated the clever little plan.

They got him in the end, of course – when he was ready and

not before. But he hadn't changed his line; he still wanted everybody in. He still wouldn't stand having anyone treated like dirt.

Nowadays we make a big deal out of the abuse that often falls on the missionary who preaches Christ's line. As if anyone can be Christ to the world without running up against the same things he encountered. As if Peter or Paul or the others had it smooth all the way. As if telling the world the gospel was a passport to instant popularity. It's not and it never was and it's not going to be. Don't let's fool ourselves.

God could take the stones and raise them up as the children of Abraham. He could – but he won't. The way Christ showed us to fill the kingdom is the way it's going to be done. And if it puts us under suspicion or opens traps and pitfalls before us maybe that's too bad – but maybe what was good enough for Christ ought to be good enough for us.

> Why not be a missionary?

Crying out loud ...

(December 1973)

Many are ever so certain that the boom in priestly and religious vocations is past. And look at all the statistics and cold water they can produce to prove it and dampen everyone's ideals. The sociological reasons for the decline and fall have been flogged to death.

Some even suggest that the missions are finished and that they were hardly ever necessary anyway, since God has his own ways of bringing people to himself. You'll find, too, a growing tendency to play down the value and importance of the priesthood and the vocation to religious life, and to argue that the lay apostolate of social service, particularly to material needs of underprivileged people, is *a more excellent way*.

And, anyway, looking at the past now with the mind of the present, it's easy enough to pinpoint all the missionaries' mistakes (and a nice cheap exercise for an armchair expert!). They could have done better: of course they could, if there hadn't been so many gaps in their training, or if Africa had stood still, or if they could have had foresight at the beginning, or if they had had a little time for survey and assessment and reflection. As a certain great man said: 'If you say nothing, and if you change nothing; then, by God, you'll make no mistakes.'

But you have to hand them this. They didn't leave things as they were. They did something in Africa that had been a long time waiting for doing. And Africa will never be the same.

Because 'from the very beginning, the Lord Jesus called to him men of his own choosing ... and he appointed twelve that they might be with him, and that he might send them forth to preach.' The Vatican Council could still say that 'missionary activity is nothing else and nothing less than a display or epiphany of God's will, and the fulfilment of that will in the world and in world history.' It could say, this same Council, that 'the Church is aware that there still remains a gigantic missionary task for her to accomplish. For the gospel message has not yet been heard, or scarcely so, by two billion human beings. And their number is increasing daily.'

Perhaps we shouldn't worry about the two billion? Most will

succeed in forgetting them, body and soul. Even though Christ so arranged the ministry of his apostles, *that both they and the Spirit were to be associated in effecting the work of salvation always and everywhere.* Maybe the rich young man of the gospel who said, *No!* to his vocation – maybe he turned out to be a great social worker. We just don't know. Let's hope he did. But you don't fulfil a vocation to priesthood or religious life by being an apostolic layman. And you don't *carefully foster and cultivate* your son's, or your brother's, priestly vocation by encouraging or urging him to be a holy and apostolic layman. We think it's time somebody started saying this out very loud.

Why not be a missionary?

Fair-weather friends

(June/July 1974)

'You're not really going back there?' the apostles protested. 'Not right now, not till the dust settles?' *But he was.* 'Well, we all think you shouldn't. Look, they tried to kill you the last time. They still want your blood. Leave it for a while, can't you, until things cool off?' *But he was bent on it, they couldn't persuade him.* 'So, right,' said Thomas, 'there's no changing him, he's going. We'd better go along.' 'Yes, and they'll kill us too,' someone argued. 'So, right, we get killed,' said Thomas, 'but we're not going to let him take off on his own, and that's for sure.'

They trailed along, the whole rattled group, *in a daze,* the gospel says, and one of them was making quiet arrangements to get out from under before the roof fell in. They knew themselves they weren't going to be much good in a crisis. It was plain he knew well enough he couldn't depend a lot on them when the crunch came. 'But don't you worry,' said Peter, 'I'll be right in there beside you whatever happens. If it's prison, they can lock up the two of us. If it's worse than that, we'll go down together. I'm sticking by you.'

He meant it, you have to give him that. And he did put up a fight when they were surrounded, even if his aim wasn't the best. But he wasn't allowed to fight the only way he knew, and it was the middle of the night and scary, so if his nerve broke for a minute when he felt they were ganging up on him, who are you to be contemptuous about it! 'No, I'm not one of that crowd, you're mistaken Miss,' said Peter. 'What? Oh no, of course I've seen him around, here and there; never met him though. Now look Miss, my accent's none of your business. Dammit; I've told you I don't know this man, and that's it, get it?' And that was it. Then, leaving him, they all fled. Nicodemus made a mild protest in his favour when the council discussed how they'd dispose of Christ, but the others turned on him and he shut up. Joseph of Arimathea declared for him when it was all over and saw he was buried decently.

Only the women stood firm. But women don't count, do they!

Afterwards, Peter and Thomas and the others remembered.

They had to live with this for the rest of their days. Peter's tears wore furrows in his cheeks, they say, the memory was so bitter. It kept coming back to them, what he'd said. 'Don't be afraid of them. What I say to you in the dark, tell in the daylight; what you hear in whispers, proclaim it from the housetops. If anyone declares himself for me in the presence of men, I will declare myself for him in the presence of my Father in heaven …'

Christ was the man to be with in the great days, when the multitudes were fed and the sick healed and the devils sent scampering. When power went out from him and the dead were raised to life. When people said, he's great, never did man speak like this man. Then you got a share in the popularity. Then they thought you were someone.

But it's not always a popular thing to be on the side of Christ. When you stand for the things he stands for and shout it from the housetops, often enough you won't get a good press. Often enough the general public doesn't want to know. Doesn't want to hear what Christ's stand is. And doesn't want to be reminded.

When you're a priest you're a constant reminder. You declare for him in the presence of men. Whether they like it or not – and when they don't you'll *know*. And when you know they don't – you have to stand firm anyway, as the women did, and as the apostles spent the rest of their lives wishing *they* had. The women, you'll remember, got all the messages on resurrection morning. *They* hadn't left any doubt which side they were on.

Why not be a missionary?

The heart of the matter

(August/September 1974)

'Good morning, fellow traveller,' I say to the man beside me. We grope for the two parts of our seatbelts, experiment with the buckles to find how they work, snick them into the locking position and tighten up the slack. 'Are you a traveller who likes to talk, or do you prefer to be left alone? – it's okay with me either way, but seeing we have half a continent to travel beside each other we may as well settle it here at the beginning.' This helps him to unfreeze and he laughs. 'A bit of both maybe?' he suggests. He'd like to read for part of the time, and I have some writing to do. While the take-off routine goes on we find out about each other, or at least I find a few basic facts on him; tourist, Norwegian, heading home after a package holiday in Mauritius, loaded with colour photographs and satisfied.

Somewhere over Rhodesia he realises he's been doing most of the talking. He grins apologetically. 'Now, about you,' he says, 'What are you? What do you do?' And I say, 'I'm a priest.' I could go on to give the peripheral details, but his reply is quick. 'I know,' he says, 'but what *do* you do?' I consider it a small minute. And I say, 'Well, to give you the kernel of it, I offer sacrifice.' He waits, totally uncomprehending, interested.

Very early this morning before I started for the airport, I stood at an altar holding a small wafer of bread and I offered it to God. Then I took a little wine in a special cup and I offered that to him as well. You'll wonder why God should want either of these things from me, seeing that he gave me both of them in the first place. Actually it was my necessity, not his. Everything I have came from him, so really there is nothing I give him – except myself. But food and drink mean my life. I've got to have them to stay alive. So what I was saying in fact was: 'My life is yours, I depend on you totally for everything, every breath, every separate heartbeat.' I believe I owe my creator this acknowledgement.

Hours later, over Libya, I was still talking, he was still listening. And asking for more. When we said goodbye at Fiumicino Airport outside Rome, he was kind enough to say he wished we were both going on together another continent or two. Well, I didn't know how much he had understood of what I'd said or how he estimated it, but he had asked a straight question, and I had tried to telescope for him all I'd ever learned, believed and experienced about being a priest. I hadn't got any writing done, nor he any reading, but we had been right through the story of creation, incarnation, redemption, and the prospects in the life to come, and we had considered what the whole thing means in the context of today. Because, I found, you can't explain about being a priest unless you bring all these things into the account.

'And you intend to spend all your life at this?' the man asked at the end. 'Right to the last breath,' I told him. 'You're not going to have much time to yourself then, I guess.' 'No, but I didn't take on this for myself.' 'You're convinced it's necessary for – well, other men?' 'I'm certain it is.' He considered for a while. 'Well, look, from what you've told me I think I understand why you do it and why you – stay with it. But now, I am heading home to my wife and children and I can share Mauritius with them, and it's great to be coming home to the welcome they'll have for me; what I'm wondering is what are you going home to?' 'I suppose I should say to the casual company of two other men who live the same kind of life as I do for the same reasons.' 'Yes, but what's *in* it for you? What do you *get* out of it?' 'I'll tell you in one word – Happiness.'

Beyond the courtesies of leave-taking there was no more to say.

Why not be a missionary?

Your witness

(October 1974)

You stand there in the little crypt, looking through the bars into a lighted cell. You hope that when they come, the thousands and millions of them, for the Holy Year of '75, they won't miss this. You'd like that they might stand here, each one alone for a little while, all by himself, looking into the rough-plastered little barred room where that man of principle named Paul, that man of compassion, of many words, of argument and tenderness and great heart, spent his last hours all those hundreds of years ago. And then went out with them to the place a little below, along that very pavement where the worn cobbles still lie stripped that he walked on, using the last minutes to say, this one final time, what he had been saying in season and out of season all the way along since his student days.

You hope they'll come here, after the basilicas, to this flaking, ancient run-down place among the eucalyptus trees, where Paul's head rolled and the long road ended that began a world away outside the gates of Damascus in a flash of blinding light.

You read the plaque, then, on the wall of the crypt. You try to grasp, to understand, to come to terms with what it means. In three languages it says it, so there should be no mistake. Here at this spot, ten thousand, two hundred and three Christian soldiers, having been forced to build the Baths of Diocletian, suffered martyrdom for the faith.

It's the *three* that gets to you. The early Christians kept the count carefully. Not losing sight of the individuals who made up the thousands. Each soldier decided for himself. In this he was all alone. The moment might have come, perhaps, in the great barracks in ancient Ostia, twenty miles away. On one of those crisp clear Italian mornings when it felt so good to be alive. Each soldier stepping in turn out of the massed ranks to make that gesture of divine worship – to a god or a goddess or to the emperor. And, a Christian soldier couldn't do it. And when he didn't, he couldn't hope that it would escape the officer's notice. Ten thousand, two hundred and three, each one all alone in his moment of testing, decided to die for their faith. And so to forced labour on the Baths of Diocletian. And on then to this place called Tre Fontane to the savage massacre.

You hope they'll come here, in from the world of noise and satellites, of money and ambition and television and so many things that do not really matter. Because here a man may find bedrock. Here he may be shattered by a sudden understanding of what it means to believe what he believes. And of what it can sometimes demand.

With his feet on Paul's old pavement, a man might easily be convinced that the faith those soldiers died for is too precious either to throw away or to hoard to himself. And that road which began outside Damascus might stretch many a mile yet.

Why not be a missionary?

Men full grown

(January/February 1975)

I once knew a man who loved a boat. A fourteen-foot beauty with sweet fast lines, blue-grey, red seats and trim. It was always moored by a chain and padlock among the flaggers in a bog stream back from the big lake. He was not poor, this man, but the thing most precious to him was the boat.

I'll never know why, but when I was a youngster growing up he lent me that lovely boat summer after summer. He'd take down the beautiful polished oars from the pins on his kitchen wall whenever I came and asked, and root out the padlock key from a dresser-drawer. Then he'd tell me what weather to expect and send me on my way. Not once did he tell me to be careful. Never a warning not to break an oar. No threats about what he'd do to me if I scratched his paint.

He knew I loved the lake. He certainly knew I was crazy about the boat. That seemed to be enough recommendation for him. Unless you love a lake or a boat, I don't think you'll understand. Unless you've sat cramped and chilled in the reeds in September dusks waiting for the mallards to come in, just to watch them and hear the splash of their arrival, with no gun, no thought of shooting them …

My friend at the lake was quite a bit like Christ. Christ was at home in boats. He was easy with men who were happy in boats. There was that understanding between him and them that you couldn't explain or describe. A kind of silent language. He didn't have to reason or argue with Peter and Andrew when he wanted them to come with him. He just called them, and they came out of that boat and followed him. They left everything there as it was, nets, lines, sails, oars, and the boat bobbing at its moorings. The lake, too, of course: don't forget the lake.

If I weren't so far away I'd still go back to my old bog stream at the lake every time I had a spare moment. If you want an argument that Christ was really a man among men, look what he did with his time off. There wasn't much of it, but whenever he and the apostles took a free day, next thing you knew they were all contentedly in a boat skimming across towards a quiet shore. Maybe just to watch the mallards coming in at dusk, who knows!

A lot of things changed after the resurrection, but not this. When they made a date to meet, where do you think it was? Not nearby on the Mount of Olives. Not out in Bethany with the Lazarus family. No, but miles away, back, you might say, at the old stand, in Galilee, on the lakeshore.

A monk I came across once, convalescing away from his abbey, told me the hardest thing for him about becoming a Cistercian was leaving his violin behind him. When I borrowed a violin for him he played for hours, badly at first because he was out of practice, then beautifully, as he got his touch back. Afterwards he smiled with great happiness and gave the instrument back to me with no dramatics at all. This was a kind of toy, however much beloved. He knew he could do without it.

Peter once asked Christ whether there would be a reward for the apostles. 'We have left *all things* and followed you.' Christ *knew* exactly how much they had left. He answered the question with great seriousness, in great detail. He knew, Christ did, how grown men can miss their toys, but he still treated them like grown men. No unnecessary warnings, no fussy instructions as if they were children. Just: 'Go out *into the whole world* and bring the *good news* to every creature.' A grown man should know how.

Why not be a missionary?

Taking for granted

(May 1975)

The windsock bellied and lifted at last and I said, 'This looks like it now,' but in a moment it went limp again. We sat in the little plane waiting, glancing at our watches. 'A breeze nearly always gets up after three,' the pilot had said. Today we needed it badly to help us get off the ground, because we had maximum load. Four persons, including one very sick, and essential baggage. It was after four. Going to be tight enough. We had to be home with enough light to make a landing.

Twenty minutes more of nothing, and then the sock lifted to the horizontal and held steady. We had our breeze. We used up all the runway there was, but we got into the air. In the back the doctor was calming down the terrified patient while we climbed in slow circles gaining height to clear the first mountain range. Business then with the radio when we levelled off. Control couldn't hear us, but a TWA captain passing far above offered to report for us. We heard him do it, making heavy weather of the multi-syllable local placenames. Now if we disappeared, they'd know roughly where to look for us.

With the very last of the light, the pilot found the landing strip and lined up to come straight in. It would happen! – a woman went chasing her child across the runway just as we were about to put down. I judged they'd have passed out of danger before we reached the place, but the pilot said 'No, we can't take a chance,' and off we went again in a roaring climb. And now we were in trouble. When we came round again it was full dark. The nearest airport with lights was two hundred miles away.

We circled – apparently there was an arrangement for this kind of emergency. The lights of a vehicle moved, down below, then the lights of another. We watched while they got into position, both facing the same way, and what looked like a short space between them. That space would be the landing strip. They flashed when they were ready for us, and we came straight for them keeping a shade to the right of the line they made. All that was called for now was a cool steady nerve, an ocean of experience, and certainly a prayer.

'Not bad, Sister,' I said to the pilot as we taxied, 'you didn't bounce – much.' I could afford to be facetious now. 'How is the patient?' she asked the doctor. 'Which one?' I said, 'I think I'm all right except for a heart attack.'

But, I thought, for these two the patient has been the priority all the time, the whole point of the journey. The unflustered dramatics of flying were never more than incidental. This had been no joyride, but just a part of the day's work. An item in a life given to service, with all the risks and hardships built-in and casually accepted.

And these were only two. Across the world there were hundreds of thousands of women like these, some religious sisters, some not, some aged or ageing, some not yet out of their teens. All of them spending all their days doing things for other people, making life better for them. Steady under stress. Efficient without ever being hard-boiled. Making it look easy when they endured beyond the bounds of generosity, or even of reason sometimes. Giving and giving, and happily being taken for granted.

The rest of us talk wisely about what needs to be done to fix the world. They are out there, and all around us – doing it!

Why not be a missionary?

High matters in a low key

(June/July 1975)

The bishop was new. The seminary was empty. What priests there were in the diocese, and there weren't many, were getting old. It was an old Catholic diocese with a good enough past. It could still tick over for a few years, just about. But to give it a future and to put life back into it, evidently something had to be done about priests. The bishop said his prayers and did some thinking. This, by the way, is a true story, from our own time.

The bishop said to himself, I can go outside the diocese, outside the country if need be, I can beg or borrow priests to keep this place going. But, he decided, that is one thing I am not going to do. He said, this diocese is a community with plenty of Catholic families. It ought to be able to supply its own needs. If it is not willing to supply its own priests, why should it expect other communities to supply them?

So he went to the families and put it to them that way. He called the young men together in the parishes, talked to them informally over soft drinks and sandwiches. He told them, we have a problem. We, that is, this community and I, its bishop. We're running out of priests. In ten years time we will be gravely short; in twenty years when your children are growing up, there will be no priests at all to take care of them. Unless we do something now.

Most of you, he told the young men, have the necessary qualities. You are sufficiently healthy, you have brains enough to absorb the knowledge a priest must have, and if you offer yourselves for the priesthood because the community needs priests, that is a perfectly good motive. Go home now and think about it, since it is evident that it is mainly on you young men of the community that the responsibility rests. Family responsibilities will make it impossible for some of you to be priests, or there may be other insuperable obstacles. But some of you will certainly find that you are free, and from this group, let those who are also *willing* come back to me. From those who are willing we will find our priests.

It was, as you see, all quite undramatic. No visions in the night. No pious ten-year-olds building sweet little shrines in the woods. No shining angels whispering inspirations in the ear. No *voices* from the tabernacle or from the statue in the corner. No gentle knocking at the door of the heart. Just a plain workaday bishop putting straight facts about responsibility. Our responsibility.

And it was enough. God, as the bishop knew, would not wish the community to run out of priests. God had seen to it that there should be a sufficiency in the community of young men with the necessary basic qualities. And it turned out that when it was put to them, enough of these young men were willing to put their lives at the service of the community, as priests. The bishop accepted those who offered themselves on a trial basis at first, obviously; and sent them to the seminary for their training. To test and be tested, you might say. Most of them survived the course. The bishop called them formally to Holy Orders eventually. Now the community is alive again and its Christian future is not in doubt. Its families continue to supply candidates for the priesthood in sufficient numbers; and now, too, the *extra* ones to bear the faith abroad, as a Christian community must.

A true story from our time, and worth telling, even if it is undramatic. Because what it illustrates, stripped down to the bare bones, is the meaning of an honest word that is too often misunderstood. The word *vocation*.

Why not be a missionary?

The boss's eye

(August/September 1975)

He was pretty sure of himself, the young man leading the close-bunched riders out through the city gate. Everyone knew he was setting out on an important mission. If you thought it was a cruel mission, you kept the thought to yourself. This young man, sitting on his horse straight and angry, could be dangerous. And the times were tense.

If you asked who he was, there were plenty willing to tell you. You're looking at the white hope of the law school, the student prodigy all the Mr Bigs talk about at the academic dinners. He's been coming up fast for a while back. Now, I guess you could say he has arrived. This mission he's going on clinches it.

The interesting thing is that he's not from one of the good city families. His roots are in a provincial town quite a way out. No, what he's got, he's made it on merit. He's brilliant, hard-working, keen. A special pet of the big professor, but that's something he had to earn. In fact, they all like him, and now it seems they trust him, too. This young man has kept his nose clean. Never once put a foot wrong. Toes the party line as though he had drawn it himself! Well, that's how you make friends and influence people in this goshawful pious-mouthed town. It's how you catch the boss's eye.

And it was true. Young Saul (otherwise Paul) was headed straight for the top of the profession. He was no pushover. It would take something very big to deflect him. But something bigger than he had ever imagined hit him like a thunderbolt, entering another city at the end of the journey he was now starting. It threw him from his horse and blinded him. And there ended, forever, all his professional ambitions. When he got his sight back, he knew that indeed he had caught the boss's eye, but that the boss was not Gamaliel, the great old professor. The boss was God. And the life's work that God had set out for him was not at all the sort of life he had spent his student years preparing for. It was something else again.

How did he feel about it? It's a fair guess that he felt like a man with a late vocation! Because that is what he was. Like one born out of due time, is how he described it himself. Did he mean that his generation seemed to have gone on ahead of him and that he now had to try to catch up? That he felt pretty lonely, a shade embarrassed, somehow badly-fitting and clumsy? That would make sense. So he dropped out of sight for three whole years, maybe trying to adjust himself, certainly doing the homework he needed to catch up.

But when he came back on the scene, he was doing no apologising for himself. The old sureness was back. His programme was clear in his mind. It was the old qualities, his sense of responsibility, capacity for hard work, sincerity, common sense, courage, directness and honesty, that won him the respect of his senior colleagues, and soon enough put him up there among the leaders. So that now when we mention Peter, the next name that naturally comes up is Paul! As well as that, his original training did not have to be written off; he found a way to put most of the things he had learned to good use.

What happened to Paul, or something very like it, could happen to you. When you've *made it* in your business, profession, job, or calling, and experienced the delights of success, it may be the thought will come that you'd like more from life than programming computers, running the department, drafting codicils, selling consumables, writing opinion columns, tracking down criminals, or breeding prize cattle. If that happens, it may indicate merely that you're not getting job satisfaction and that you're bored. But it could be the first warning that a thunderbolt is going to strike you, and you're going to have to take a totally new direction in order to be at peace. To some men (and these are not usually the failures or the pushovers) the priesthood is the only answer once they've caught the boss's eye.

Why not be a missionary?

Friendship's risks

(March 1976)

Now there is in Jerusalem by the Sheep Gate, a pool, in Hebrew called Bethzatha, which has five porticos ... So begins the half-page story of a man who, one ordinary day like any other day, found himself face to face with Christ. Thirty-eight years sick and helpless, one of a *multitude* of blind, lame and paralysed, counting the porticos, one, two, three, four, five, over and over, a million times, because there was nothing else to do. And then, this ordinary day like any other day, Christ there beside him. Christ saying, 'See, you are well, get up and walk!'

Walking then, walking, walking; so wonderful just to walk. Learning how to live when there was no longer pain! Quailing at the snags, problems, challenges, that being well again began at once to introduce. Struggling for courage to live without dependence. Finding probably that there were other kinds of pain ...

How did he handle things afterwards, the man from the pool by the Sheep Gate? How did Lazarus fare after having been raised from the dead? What became of the scribe who offered to follow Christ and got that off-putting reply about the foxes and the birds? Did the rich young man get richer or go bankrupt?

Well, no one knows. But when a man comes face to face with Christ, it is certain things are not the same again. Life gets new meanings. There are new delights, perhaps also unexpected anguishes. Tough tasks may have to be confronted, strong decisions to be made, fears to be faced down, self-interest to be emptied out. There will be call for some sort of commitment, maybe even for a lifetime commitment, and a man must answer *yes* or *no*. That's when a man is tempted to take to the hills, to run. But it's not that easy. There was a whale to bring Jonah back when he ran. You could say every man has his own personal whale, deep inside him.

When you come face to face with Christ, it is then that you really grasp for the first time that he is not a harmless formless general kind of *presence* found only in church sanctuaries. He is another person, flesh and blood and spirit and divinity, reaching to you, claiming a personal relationship, claiming friendship, trust, brotherhood, claiming love, claiming all you've got, offering

FRIENDSHIP'S RISKS

all he's got to you. When Christ visits you like that, you know something's got to be done about it. He is not playing games.

And he'll be back. Unless your response is a flat and definite *no* (or perhaps *even* if it is) he will be back. Different ways, different times. In the street, the church, the crowd, the desert. When and how he chooses. Reaching you through what you hear, read, see, remember, flashing light into your understanding, presenting ideas to your awareness, bringing vital things into sharp focus. You'll know he has been there, sometimes. As the quiet deep dialogue develops, you will come to understand that really he has never been away.

But isn't it risky, letting this thing develop into a close deep friendship? Who knows where it may lead? How can you know what Christ may ask of you – a lifetime commitment maybe – to goodness, to marriage, to religious life, to the priesthood, to celibacy, to service, to sanctity? How do you know you'll be able to give what he demands?

Oh yes, you take a risk. That is where trust enters in. And he takes a bigger risk, having anything to do with you! He, you see, knows just what you're made of – he remembers that you are dust!

One thing, though, he will not hit you with everything at once. He will lead you along gradually, building up your strength and generosity before every demand. And another thing: as long as you stay close, you will not fail him at the crunch points. He will not let you.

Why not be a missionary?

The edge of survival

(April 1976)

Shovelfuls of dirt were coming up out of the hole in the dry bed of the river. I could see just the top of the young priest's head, which meant he was down eight or nine feet. I wondered what time he had got up. It was very early in the morning, out in the middle of the desert, and the top rim of the sun was just appearing. 'Hi!' I said, 'good morning down there.' 'Go away – I'm busy.' He had second thoughts – 'No, get another shovel and scrape back some of that stuff from the lip, it's falling back in on me.' 'To dig I am not able – and it's not nice to ask me, I'm a visitor.' He said something impolite. I went and got a shovel.

He was preparing to lay a pipeline. One end of the pipe would reach down into the water trapped under the sand on the hard bed; the other would connect with a tap several hundred yards away in a nomad camp. In between, a small petrol engine would drive a pump. 'Did you know,' I asked him, 'that you are making a contribution to integral human development?' 'I'll take your word for it,' he said, 'they didn't teach me that kind of language at school.' I pressed him … 'Well, would you call it – pre-evangelisation?' 'No, I'd call it amateur plumbing – very amateur.'

He climbed out of the hole, sweat evaporating off him in the tinder dry air. He was wearing only a dusty pair of khaki shorts and was brown to the bone all over. 'You and your big words,' he grumbled, 'What I'm simply at is saving these folk the bother of digging ten feet of sand away every time they want to get water for themselves or their camels. They haven't that much energy to spare. They've put two major famines over them in the past three years.'

He drank water from a bottle, sat down on the sand and lit a cigarette. 'Pre-evangelisation,' he reflected, 'well, I suppose you've got to start somewhere. These are great, hardy, austere-living people. The principal business of their lives is survival, just that. We strangers, even we don't live so high; our food comes from two hundred miles away. If a guest comes without notice, everyone goes short. If the lorry breaks down on the road, we don't eat. Teaches you the basics of living, a little water, just enough food, no fancy stuff.'

'We live like the people, hand to mouth. They're tight-knit and mistrustful of strangers, but they see us living on the edge of survival like themselves, and that makes a bond. Then, we try to get in food for them, when the rains fail, and we patch up their sick when they let us. We set up tiny industries so they can make a little money and buy in food. Maybe they wonder why we bother, but they know we're here ready to serve them. When they get to asking us why, that's our opening to get on the subject of the Christian gospel. Meanwhile, you may have noticed that we desert rats spend a lot of our time praying.' (I had noticed!) 'The desert helps you to pray, you know.' (He grinned.) 'None of us set out to be contemplatives originally, but to make any missionary sense, when the time is not ripe for preaching, you pray instead. Penance is built-in to the life, so there you've got the two main ingredients for softening-up the target area. Is that pre-evangelisation? It's what we're doing, anyway.'

'But look,' – he glared at me – 'you mentioned, what was it – integral human development? Don't get yourself confused, buster; that monster is nothing more than what we used to call the corporal works of mercy. Feed the hungry, *et cetera,* and teach them to grow food for themselves. Visit the sick. Bury the dead. Big deal – what kind of Christian would you be if you didn't do these things! But you're a missionary and so am I, and we ought to know that if that's all a Christian's going to do, he hasn't begun to understand what the gospel is about.'

He climbed back into the hole and began shovelling. 'I have nothing against the aid agencies,' he shouted up, 'some of them send the money to keep me here. They have to do their publicity campaigns to raise that money. But I just hope the decent folk who dig into their pockets to help the agencies help me to help our friends over there in the camp don't get the idea that a bleeding heart disaster appeal is in the same category as the gospel of Jesus Christ! Christ didn't come on earth just to see that we all had full bellies.'

Why not be a missionary?

Going for broke

(June/July 1976)

'It's not right,' that was all he said. Not right to judge a man till you've heard his side of the case. Not right to condemn him till it's proved he has deserved it. It was elementary. It was the Law. But they turned on Nicodemus with a cutting jibe. Are you a Galilean too? It was a threat. They would put a label on him if he insisted.

He didn't insist. He let them get away with it. He didn't want to be labelled. And so, Christ died on a trumped-up charge. Nicodemus saw to it that he was buried decently. But that was afterwards when the big chance had passed him by.

A decent likeable man, Nicodemus, a leading Jew with all the right instincts, an honest Pharisee with a heart, a ruler of the people with a tender conscience for justice. Heart and conscience and instinct said – declare for Christ. But Christ was a *persona non grata* in the ruling circle. It would have taken a lot of courage to go overboard for him. And Nicodemus didn't have that kind of courage. He hadn't had it that other time, and he didn't have it now. Ah well.

They say he became a saint anyway – eventually. He must have realised at last that he couldn't have it both ways. He must have stopped hedging his bets, and gone for broke. So, good for him!

He was sold on Christ right from the beginning. 'No man,' he said, 'no man can do the things you do unless God is with him.' That was the night he came cautiously in out of the dark for an after-hours talk with Christ. The night he met Christ face to face (a thing no man forgets, ever). The night Christ took all the wraps off the plan of redemption and told him in extraordinary detail how God intended to save the world.

You'll find their conversation very bewildering, very tantalising. That's because the gospel gives only a sketchy account of it and leaves out most of the links. But you'll get the feeling that these two understood each other very well. Nicodemus knew what Christ was saying to him.

He must have gone home that night walking on air, not doubting any more, convinced and grateful and at peace. But he wasn't telling anybody. He was not ready to take a stand in public. Not yet. Not for a long time yet. Not until Christ's death had been already engineered by the ruling group of which he, Nicodemus, was a member. But he went to the funeral, that at least. And probably got labelled in the end anyway!

Yes, Nicodemus was a good man; a good man who might have been great. You don't want to blame him too much, but you don't want to repeat his inglorious performance in your own life, either. So face it, friend – how well does the Christian label fit *you*? Is it publicly evident from your words, deeds and attitudes that the goods under the label are not bogus? To be seen on Christ's side today, to be truly *Christian* in the stand you take regarding many a thing under current debate, can tax your courage – and earn you jibes. It can isolate you, can seem to put you in the wrong.

Yet, if you have looked Christ in the face, you may find he has been asking even more than that – from you. He does, from some people, ask the all-or-nothing gift of everything. The lifelong gift of themselves, acknowledging him always before men, *being* him to all men! To these special ones it may seem at first unreasonable, unthinkable, impossible, but they go on bravely looking Christ in the face, and they know how to say *yes*.

Why not be a missionary?

Everything fixed

(August/September 1976)

'You will go to Assisi for the *festa*?' said Eginia. It was a statement, a question and a royal command all at once. Eginia is from Umbria, Assisi is in Umbria, and all the world should go to Assisi for the *festa*. She stood over me, the teapot in one hand, a platter of *insalata* in the other, her mind on neither. In a minute, like as not, I was going to be scalded.

'There will be the traffic enormous,' I pleaded. 'It is too far to go and come in one day. With the crowd gigantic there for the *festa*, it will be for him who proposes himself to stay the night impossible to find a bed. For the motive of the inflation, then, the *benzina* is costing four hundred lire a litre …'

Her smile made little of the problems. 'Let not our sirship preoccupy itself of the lodgement. There is the Oasis of the Sacred Heart. My beloved old friend is the directress. She will provide indubitably for you a bed in the chaplain's quarters. Let us but find the number telephonic …'

There followed a fifteen-minute intercity phonecall, with many yelps of joy, reminiscences, verbal embraces, and a character reference that made even my toes blush. There would be beds for all who came. I would be treated like a cardinal. *Tutto apposto* – everything fixed!

'Do for me courteously in Assisi a favour,' said Eginia. 'Bear my fervent love to Jesus on the cross in San Damiano. That crucifix most beautiful, a work stupendous, is found in the *capella* on the right near the entrance. You will see the story written. The artist had sculptured all except the face, but at that point he was constrained to draw back in defeat, for how could a man know to recreate the inexpressible countenance of Jesus crucified! That night he went home dejected to pray and sleep, but in the morning, lo! – the impossible task had been completed by an *unknown hand*.'

'It is a face most marvellous. Contemplated from directly in front, it is of unspeakable majesty. Regarded from the right, it has the aspect of a human being, a man like the rest of men, you understand, and suffering indescribably. But let your sirship then but direct its gaze from the left, and there is found yet again another diverse impression; the face of one suffering, it is true, but suffering with such serenity, such sweetness, such embracing love, that it seems to claim to itself all the *tristezza,* the *amarezza,* the sorrow, the bitterness of your whole life, making it sweet also, supportable and serene. You know most certainly that Jesus shares your pain, and that he confides to you his own pain for all the world.' The face of the tough capable Eginia, who spends her life sharing the pain of other people, was tender and tearful, remembering.

In the end, I was not able to go to Assisi for the *festa,* but now I know I must go soon, because Eginia's story continues to haunt me. Like any of the thousand legends in marvel-strewn Italy, it could be true, and anyway it is beautiful. And if that *face,* whether carved by man or angel, has something to tell me of the thoughts of the dying Saviour, surely into Umbria I must go.

It is because of what happened on the cross that any priest is a priest. Because of it, he has *good news* to tell the world, and pardon, hope and sacrament to offer it. *Tutto apposto,* in other words, everything fixed ... and that *is* the *good news* in a nutshell.

Why not be a missionary?

Pills in the garbage

(October 1976)

Two girls whispering. One radiant-faced, the other with a pallor of stunned grief. 'He's come,' the first one says, 'he wants you; you're to go out to him there away from all these people …'

He waited on the road, out beyond the outskirts of the village, strangely reluctant now to go farther. He would have no words of formal comfort for them, no carefully assumed funeral face for the benefit of watching mourners. It would be enough that he was there, that he had come. There was already so much between him and them, so close a relationship of trust and friendship, that empty formality was unthinkable.

Watching Martha running to fetch her sister, he must have been remembering the evening when she had complained to him about her. It wasn't in Martha, really, he knew, to be catty, jealous or vindictive. It was only that she saw hungry men to be fed and knew all the practical things that had to be done to feed them. To her mind, there would be plenty of time for easy conversation after the coffee had been served. So she complained about her inactive sister, as will happen in any family, and the guest himself was not excluded from the blame.

And Martha had got no support. What she had got was a suggestion, affectionate but perfectly clear, that she ought to take another look at her priorities. Did she flounce away disgustedly with her armful of plates and cutlery? Did she exclaim *m-e-n!* in that tone of voice an exasperated woman will use, banging things around in the kitchen? Maybe indeed she did, and Christ would have smiled with rueful understanding.

But Martha knew, as had just now appeared here on the road, that the guest was more than just *man*. Certainly she would have given thought to what he had said. Calmed down, she would quite probably have left sinkfuls of dirty crockery to wait, while she joined Mary in her conversation with Christ …

There has got to be time for this, always – time for being quiet with Christ – and let no Christian claim that in the twenty-four hours of the day he *cannot* find a slot for it. Five minutes, ten, fifteen: it is not so much the length of time that is vital. What really counts is that the giving of one's self to it should be total: that this should be Christ's time and nothing and nobody else's. For this is more important than finishing a page, or getting out a Monday washing at half past three, or being there dead on time at the corner to meet the boys.

It is a daily therapy of which we all have great need. We are, each of us, alone in a disturbing time and a confusing crowd: in sore need of comfort, understanding and reassurance. Yes, and of much more than this, often enough. We need to know we can reach out any time and touch the hem of Christ's garment. We need to hear him say to us, even when we know it already – that we are healed.

We have to listen for that, but we cannot listen unless we make quiet around us, and quiet within us. Yes, it takes effort to shake the mind free and concentrate it totally on Christ. And it takes practice too. But the effort pays off, for there will be moments when the mind focuses in undivided attention; when, you might say, our eyes lock with Christ's; and it is then that the two-way communications pass back and forth, that insecurity vanishes, that the healing we need reaches deep into the core of us. Then the pilgrim can turn his face resolutely to the world again, sure of his direction, refreshed and renewed for the next stage of the long march home. Ready for anything.

So many boxes of drugs and pills, so many tranquillisers and stimulants, so many painkillers we could throw out with the garbage ... if we would just take this medicine and take it daily. So many heart attacks would never happen, so many psychiatric wards would close down for want of customers, so many troubled marriages would straighten out, so many mixed-up young people would find understanding and peace, so many broken hearts would know happiness again. If all of us, *all of us,* could find a little time every day to be with Christ. And how many empty seminaries would soon be filled again with people who want to give everything for always ... for daily personal time with Christ is the answer to so many of the things that trouble us. And it is the only answer ...

He is waiting out there away from the crowds, as Martha told Mary. He wants you. He is calling for you. The results, if we choose to go to him, can be spectacular. But no one is going to carry us.

Why not be a missionary?

The cutting edge

(November 1976)

Somewhere a few miles to the right, the map said, was the Zaire border. Somewhere ahead there should be a big industrial city. But here, where the minibus bowled along the smooth tarred road, there was just drab mile upon mile of long parched grass and not a living being in sight, neither animal nor man. Nothing like a landmark anywhere. Not a single thing to interest the eye.

And it was here – where? – that the driver murmured something about visiting his family. He turned off the road, straight into the long brown grass, up and over a bank, and with nothing at all to prepare us for it, we were instantly in the middle of three hundred thousand people. It was a kind of shanty town, neater than you'd expect, with trim small houses reaching street upon street, block upon block, as far as the eye could see.

You'll say this is contrived, maybe, but it isn't at all. That big city of small houses was totally hidden in the grass. And that instant passage from unpeopled wilderness to swarming pulsing community brought up something else unexpected. It brought up a picture of Christ with his apostles, and of Christ saying a shocking thing: Christ making a statement – with a conclusion that didn't seem to follow. All power is given *to me* – therefore go *you* and make disciples of all men.

Had they heard, had anyone told them, these hundreds of thousands in this unmapped city in the grass? Had anyone brought *them* the *good news* that Christ charged his apostles to carry to earth's end? Was it being told and re-told among them, celebrated, pondered, flashed into active creative reality in daily living?

And the answer, as very soon appeared, was *yes,* triumphant, resounding *yes.* The word had come. To this community, as to many another far more remote. As it had come, long ago, or only the other day, to the little lost villages in steaming forests, in almost inaccessible pockets in the mountains, and out on the floor of deserts without end.

The story can end here, of course. This generation can celebrate the past, can congratulate itself that so much has already been done, can say: 'Let us now praise famous men – and rest easy.' And doing thus, can be forever shamed, forever labelled as a Christian generation in decline.

Christ's shocking charge still stands; *will* stand until the work is done; till all men are made disciples, till they are his followers, his men. But the *good news* that makes men his disciples is carried on two feet; on the feet of individual men and women who care enough to put other things aside, so that they may leave themselves free to carry it.

The generation just now passing into old age bred a great many such men and women. Will the new generation prove to have produced as many again? It could, and they can – probably must – be greater than ever came out of the past.

                Why not be a missionary?

The frozen people

(January/February 1977)

A very charming lady sat talking across a desk to me about a job she had to do. She was a producer in the religious department of a television station, and she was putting a programme together for a date several months ahead. It would get forty minutes, she said, in the *God-slot* on a Sunday. She explained that the *God-slot* was station jargon for the period allotted to religious programming on any given day.

I thought about it. A television service tries to cater for all kinds of tastes. There would be time-slots for sport, women's affairs, arts, politics, agriculture, economics, pop, and so on. Naturally, there would be a slot for God. Lots of people are interested in God.

All right, maybe, for a television station. For you, though, it won't do. Not Sunday. Not any day. You can't confine God to one slot in your life, and exclude him from all the rest of it. You can't just pay him formal attention at Sunday Mass, and tell yourself that that's him taken care of for the week. You can't throw him a gabble of hurried prayers morning and evening, and go about the day's affairs as if they had nothing to do with him.

Well, you *can*, but you mustn't. If that is the way you deal with God, don't you think you are being a little hard on *yourself* (and on everyone else, of course)? Look, could we just leave God's side of this out of our considerations for a moment – if you like, leave him in his *slot* out of the way – and think of what you're doing to *yourself*?

I remember a very rough day years ago when I had a crowd of angry people around the house for hours looking for a lot of money that I didn't have. It was pay day for teachers and I owed them the money, so they had a right to be angry. Well, I could have saved myself a lot of grief if I had looked a little more attentively at a flimsy three-inch-square slip of paper on the office table under my nose. It was a voucher entitling me to draw seven thousand pounds from the provincial treasury down the road. That slip of paper was just what I needed to bring smiles to every face, including my own. And I didn't know it was there. It didn't look valuable, so I'd missed it.

Now, there was a day in your life when you became a member of God's household; the day you were *born again;* the day of your baptism. You got a large handful of treasury vouchers that day, and they entitled you, permanently, to various enrichments which could make your daily life ever so much more agreeable. It is really up to you whether you draw what you are entitled to, or pass it up. You can leave it lying in the treasury if that's the way you feel about it, and it will still be safely unused the day you die. It won't have done you any good, and you can't take it with you. Nobody else will have got any advantage from it, either, but that will be the least of your concerns, because by then your own heart will have dried up inside you, and you won't have a thought for anybody but yourself. Also, you won't like yourself very much.

But what a way for Christ's brother or sister to live! In a mean succession of dreary days without meaning or fulfilment! Life should give more than that. There ought to be joy, hope, always a profound interior peace, security, confidence, happiness, tranquillity, even when life is dealing you heavy body-blows. There ought to be courage to meet all the threats, and sureness for every grave decision. There ought to be faith, unshaken and unshakeable, when the doubters or scoffers challenge what a man believes. There ought to be strength when pleasure or profit search out his weakness. There ought to be a steel jacket around his integrity ...

And there will be, too – as well as all the time in the world to take care of other people – when you live the length of each day in close touch with God.

Why not be a missionary?

My face like flint

(April 1977)

My colleague from northern Europe seemed a little nervy and withdrawn this morning, and I thought I knew why. This evening he sets off on a journey to the far side of the world. Fine if it were for a holiday, but it's not. When it's a working trip with a lot depending on it and you the man in the gap. You have apprehensions and misgiving before you set out. You're withdrawn because already you feel the aloneness of being the one responsible. Also, though this is not a main consideration, it is in the back of your mind that your plane just may slice a path to the bottom of the Indian Ocean.

I said to him, 'Do you know the day you've picked to start out? It's the feast of all the saints of Ireland; good travellers all.' In his country they take the saints seriously, and the Irish saints especially, for they know them from way back. The news cheered him. 'Did they have a motto or slogan,' he asked, 'those loose-footed apostles of yours from the west, who outfaced our ancient northern gods and beat us into line?' 'They did,' I told him, 'and how do you like it? It was *peregrinare pro Christo* – to go journeying for Christ.' 'I like it well,' he smiled, 'it fits this day, it fits it very well.'

The journeys are often much longer nowadays than those tough ascetic predecessors of ours faced long ago when they set out to rescue Europe from the Dark Ages. What awaits us at the end of the journey is possibly more complex, less clear-cut, than what they expected to encounter. But their farewells on the threshold of home were usually final and forever. They did not expect to come back. In the aloneness of their going forth, did they recall, perhaps, the thrilling terrible words of Isaiah's fearless prophecy – 'For the Lord God helps me ... therefore I have set my face like flint ... I turned not backward ... and I know that I shall not be put to shame ...'?

Great words for bolstering the courage, and courage is called for, especially at the outset, when a man sets himself the commitment to spend his life journeying for Christ. There are other words, too, close by in Isaiah, that can help to swing a wavering decision to the sticking point: 'Why, when I came, was there no man? When I called, was there no one to answer? Is my hand shortened, that it cannot redeem? or, have I no power to deliver?'

And might Christ not take these words from his prophet of long ago and speak them with a fearful new signification to his people in the world today? In his very last charge before his ascension, did he not put it upon us, his followers, to carry his redemption to all peoples till the end of time? And will we now refuse the charge? Can we, perhaps, manacle his redeeming hand by our unwillingness to be instruments of redemption? Can we strangle his *power to deliver* by refusing to undertake a mission of deliverance in his name?

Was there not something in our mythology called a *geasa*, a sacred *task* laid upon a man that rested implacably upon him until it was carried out? We have such a task from Christ, and we have not yet fulfilled it, and it will remain with us. Some of us certainly must go – but who? Is there no man? Is there no one to answer?

Why not be a missionary?

How safe is safe?

(May 1977)

Mark's mother's was a *safe* house, so when the heat was on they gathered there, a group of them, to pray. Tomorrow was the day for the big show trial. Barring some kind of miracle, they could forecast the result. James' execution had been popular. Peter's would bring the house down. Peter was the leader. Herod knew. Everyone knew. In Mark's mother's house, they prayed for a miracle. They needed Peter.

The prayers were interrupted. A scream, a running girl, a gasped-out announcement. 'You're out of your mind girl,' they hushed her. 'I'm not,' she pleaded, 'please believe me – he's there at the outside door!' Yes, there was a furtive knocking. Yes, it was Peter, afraid to knock too loudly because of the passers-by on the street. He silenced them quickly, told them how he had escaped from prison, told them to pass the word around, slipped away to some safer place he knew.

'Now I know it wasn't a dream,' Peter told himself wonderingly. 'I *was* chained to two soldiers. An angel did really come and wake me up. He did knock off the chains and he did tell me to put on my shoes and belt and not to forget my cloak. He led me past the two guardposts and out through the iron door; and down the full length of a street. And then he left me. And here I am, free, and I'll have to go underground for a while.'

Only for a while, just long enough to let the storm blow over. And then, on with the job again; whatever happened, that must go on. There would be many a court to face yet, many a threat, many jails and floggings to endure. But the answer to the authorities would never vary. It would always be the same firm affirmation: 'We cannot give an undertaking to keep silent about what we have seen and heard. We are witnesses to Christ. If there is a conflict between what God expects of us and what men demand of us, we tell you straight, there can be only one outcome – we will do what God requires of us, come what may.'

They knew, Peter and the others – indeed they had proved it beyond doubt – that they were no natural heroes. They knew that their assignment called for heroism of the highest kind. They had an answer for this dilemma. They did not depend on themselves. They knew where the strength had to come from. 'And now, Lord, take note of their threats and help your servants to proclaim your message with all boldness ...' That was how they prayed. And once in a while, the house where they prayed *rocked* with the gust of the spirit's coming, and out went these craven, timid men, flaming and fortified, into the streets once more crying out the message in the teeth of the world.

There are only so many *safe* houses, and well Peter knew it. His life was on the line all through the years, and there came a fiery night in the reign of Nero when the ultimate heroism was demanded of him. So his friends buried him stealthily by night in an illegal grave, and perhaps they knew even then that by his constancy the message he had lived and died for had already spread so far that now it could never be smothered or suppressed. And a great dome rears above his grave today that points the world to heaven in a silent unwavering message that is still faithfully his message.

There are still people who lay their life on the line, they keep Peter's message, Christ's message, before the eyes of man. From some of them, the ultimate heroism is still called for, and they give it readily. Today it is Rhodesia, Uganda. Tomorrow – who knows where? To go out with the message means to accept the risks; but with a guarantee: 'He that loses his life for my sake will find it; greater love than this hath no man ...'

Why not be a missionary?

Fact and life

(August/September 1977)

A day comes round each month on which the text for this page has got to be written. Actually it is practically always written at night when it is possible to bank on an open-minded period in which there will be no interruptions because everyone is asleep. And it is always the last possible night, because that is the way casual columnists with other things to do usually have to operate. Now, because it is the last possible night and there's no time at all left for thinking about it, all kinds of alarm bells begin to ring if the great author finds himself without a single idea in his head. That is the situation tonight. But courage! Certain provisions have been made for this regularly occurring emergency. There is a file marked *Facts*. Find it, search in it and see what comes out …

Fact one: England has eight hundred people to the square mile, Holland nine hundred and forty, Taiwan nine hundred and ten. Fact two: Each year one hundred and twenty-seven million children are born, ninety-five million come to school age, nineteen million reach age sixty-five. Fact three: There are nearly four million Australians under the age of fifteen years. All items dated 1972. Out of date and not very promising. What else? Here's something dated 1263. A long time ago, yes, but still relevant. Let's try this one …

Have you heard of a place called Bolsena? A little grey stone town on a lakeshore, maybe a hundred miles to the north of Rome. Two little churches side by side in the oldest part, making one side of a small cobbled square. The Miracle of Bolsena happened in one of them in 1263. Have I turned you off? Who believes in miracles any more? I for one believe in this one. So did Pope Urban IV: he established the feast of *Corpus Christi* as a result of it. So did St Thomas Aquinas, apparently; he composed the Mass for the new feast. So do the hundreds who walk through the streets of Orvieto in stately procession each *Corpus Christi* escorting the ancient squares of stained and blackened linen, and the thousands who stand to watch them pass …

There was this priest in Bohemia who was finding it pretty difficult to believe in anything at all. His faith had become very shaky, especially his faith in the real presence of Christ in the Eucharist. He had enough faith left, however – or was it hope? – to make him decide to do something about it, and he fixed on something quite difficult and dangerous, a pilgrimage to Rome. There were no package tours in 1263, and Rome is a long way from Bohemia.

Along the way, this man stopped a night in Bolsena, and in the morning, as he said his Mass in one of the churches in the little cobbled square, the sacred host bled on the corporal. It must have bled a great deal, because the blood soaked through the cloth on to the stone of the altar table. You can still see the stains on the fragments of that altar table, now set in the wall above the present altar. And the corporal is there to be seen in its shrine in the cathedral town a few miles away.

That is the story, and after all those years it is still relevant. It ties up in a strange way with the Last Supper, which happened a long, long time earlier. It ties up with a promise made earlier still and with a flat declaration by Christ that we must eat his flesh and drink his blood in order to live. It ties up with England and Holland and Taiwan, and with all those millions who are born and reach school age and grow old, and hunger and thirst for the food and drink that does not perish. It ties up with your columnist in the night who, in a little while now, will be saying his morning Mass, holding the host in which Christ will be as really present as he was that morning long ago in Bolsena, or that night in Jerusalem. It ties up with you too, with your hungers and thirsts, with your interior life, with what you might be and what you could do.

> Why not be a missionary?

Lift the world's heart

(October 1977)

There were fifty-something programmes shown (the man said) and I sat through forty-something of them. He was just back from a television festival where producers from the various Christian Churches had been looking at their own and at each other's work and studying how to improve it.

Technically (he said) it was mostly high quality stuff. It was the content that bothered me. It seemed to me that the cumulative effect of all that programming was negative and depressing. You got the impression that the Christian producers were terribly preoccupied about reflecting *the bad conscience of humanity*. There was the poverty we hadn't relieved, the oppressive regimes we had been silent about, the internal disagreements we hadn't resolved, the injustices we had gone along with, that kind of thing. A terrible concentration on our weaknesses and our selfishness and failures. I asked myself – but is this all we have to tell the world about our rich and wonderful faith?

Is this the *good news,* this guilt-ridden exposure of our shortcomings in making Christ's dreams for us a reality? How can this inspire or attract?

I came away thinking that, great heavens, we have the certainty that God is our Father and that Christ has opened the way to him! We know without a doubt that repentance brings forgiveness, that we are invited to the wedding feast, that an eternity of unimaginable happiness is ours for the taking. We know that 'neither death nor life, nor angels, nor principalities, nor things present, nor things to come, nor powers, nor height, nor depth, nor anything else in all creation, will be able to separate us from the love of God in Christ Jesus Our Lord.' Well, then, why don't we say a lot more about this positive side of things? It ought to be more interesting, to say the least, than our petty squabbles or our mean and cowardly Christian performance.

This man was talking in generalities, giving his overall reaction to a concentrated viewing session which had tired and depressed him, and when pressed he had no difficulty in conceding that there had, in fact, been several very positive and optimistic presentations which left little cause for complaint.

But, even apart from television, didn't he have a point? A preacher of the gospel is an announcer of *good news,* and he has enough material in his faith to lift the heart of the world.

I had just written that and was casting about for a way to frame the next sentence, when my eye fell on a paragraph in the very latest thing the Pope has written about evangelisation. It says just what I was groping to say: 'Today, more than before, we see a need for zealous apostles who do not lose themselves in useless discussion or sterile questions, but who consecrate their whole life to the universal mission, sowing "not doubts and uncertainties ... but certainties that are solid because they are anchored in the Word of God".'

Solid certainties: that's what we are lucky enough to have. And what's to stop us consecrating our whole life to telling the world these certainties.

Why not be a missionary?

Taking a tranquilliser

(April 1978)

I wake up still tense with the anxieties I went to sleep with, and there is no morning offering in my mind, but only lines from a poem I read somewhere, repeating themselves meaninglessly as they must have been doing in my sleep:
There will be time, there will be time
To prepare a face to meet the faces that you meet ...

But I know there won't be time, that there hasn't been time to prepare for the heap of problems that is going to come piling on me today. So there will be oversights, mistakes, serious mishandling of people that matter and business that is important. Sloppy work, and who knows how much damage ... and even now the minutes are ticking away ...

So the tension builds. A little more of this and it is going to be the kind of day I go round in circles and end by leaving bad enough worse. It is time to take things in hand. Time to put everything aside, sit down quietly and firmly and look in God's face. Let him show me all over again how very little depends on me, after all.

First five minutes mostly forcing myself not to look at my watch, just to sit there emptying my churning mind. There was something about David in a reading yesterday that maybe I could anchor on. David – he was centuries ago! What was it? A picture comes up clearly out of the far past, a bible-history drawing. David with the huge sword, steadying himself to cut off Goliath's head.

And now I look up at God and laugh. Be patient with me – no, but it is funny, I've just found myself wondering how did David behead the giant: did he saw, or chop? With the descent into the ridiculous, the tension vanishes, and I know what it was that I was trying to remember.

David answering the jeering taunts of the Philistine, running forward, fitting one of the five smooth stones into his sling, hoarse with anger because this uncircumcised Philistine has dared insult the armies of the living God. A slip of a boy hurling himself at that enormous veteran in his armour, certain that he's going to destroy him ...

'You come against me with sword and spear and javelin, but I come against you in the name of the Lord of Hosts.'

Goliath never had a chance.

The images come quickly now, one after the other, but still somehow all together. Another great warrior, Michael the Archangel, shaking heaven with his battle cry against Lucifer: *'Who is like to God?'* A shaggy-dressed man with quiet reflective eyes, the greatest ever born of woman, John the Baptist, telling the only wish of his heart: *'He must increase, I must decrease.'* And a great artist from a later age, a man named Gian Lorenzo Bernini, whose sculptures filled a city with beauty and laughter, whose monuments to the great ones of his time still fill the world with wonder. His own monument an undistinguished slab in a church floor with an unpretentious inscription in Latin: *'Here the Bernini family await the resurrection.'*

Maybe it's a strange kind of morning prayer, but now things are back in proportion. Today is going to be possible, in spite of all. Because I don't have to be God, I only have to lean on him.

Why not be a missionary?

Sound and light

(June/July 1979)

It was a big auditorium with bare walls and terrible acoustics, but the equipment was high quality and when you put on headphones you heard comfortably. The speaker at the microphone looked a little shabby and not at all distinguished. You'd never have guessed that he was one of the top two or three authorities in his field, respected and recognised as such worldwide. His English left practically everything to be desired, and you had to listen carefully to follow what he said. His manner was unassuming, a little self-deprecatory, friendly, and you certainly wouldn't have described him as a brilliant speaker, except ... Well, except that he somehow held that audience rivetted and motionless through the length of three hour-long sessions, and that after he had left they stayed on discussing in earnest groups, until the men came to put up the shutters.

Discussing what he had said, not discussing him. That, you began to realise, was his special strength: he did not allow anything, least of all himself, to get between you and his message. Next day you could hardly remember what he looked like, but you went on being haunted by the low-key passion of his presentation; you knew that it was the anguish of his own conviction which had held that audience captive, and left them also anguished.

His theme was what he called *audio-visual man,* and his anxiety was how to get through to him with the faith. The faith remained the same, unchanging and unchangeable, but the ways of getting it to man, and man's way of receiving it, could and did change and undergo new developments. Why? Because great changes occurred in man's way of living, in his way of absorbing information, in his way of understanding. The ways of teaching, of necessity, had to be adapted so as to take account of these changes.

One of the great changes came with the invention of the printing press, five hundred years ago. Information came to us then largely on a printed page, with the ideas following one another in logical order, to be considered and reflected upon, to be absorbed, analysed, arranged neatly, and stored away in the

SOUND AND LIGHT

mind. Reason and intelligence were the active partners that did most of the work.

Print is still there, but another great invention has come in more recent times to bring a great change. Electricity, and fast on its heels, electronics. And so to amplified sounds, projected images, colours, lights, new atmospheres and sensations. And so to a world where a man of seventy-five spends nine years of his life before a television set. Absorbing his ideas now, the experts calculate, seven per cent from the words, thirty-eight per cent from the speaker's way of talking (voice, vocabulary, rhythm), and (note it!) fifty-five per cent from the speaker's gestures and movements and the expression on his face. A world where you don't ask yourself any longer what the film was about after you've seen it; you ask what has been the effect of it on you, how you *feel* after it.

It is a world in which the gospel has to be announced still. But it has to be announced to *audio-visual man;* in a language he can understand. And he who announces it must know the language.

Why not be a missionary?

Send men to Joppa

(August/September 1979)

A few days ago I met a missionary wearing somebody else's overcoat. His own was two thousand miles away, probably still draped over the seat of the car that took him to the airport in Lagos. I said to myself, 'They don't change much, do they?' I was remembering St Paul, sitting in a prison cell in Rome all those years ago, writing a letter to Timothy. 'When you come (he wrote) bring the cloak that I left at Troas, and the books, and above all the parchments ... Do your best to come before the winter.' There wouldn't have been many spare overcoats lying around in Paul's time, and reading matter wasn't very plentiful either.

But I'd love to know what Timothy said when he got that message! He was a saint, of course, and he worshipped Paul; but *still*, he was going to have to drag all that extra baggage from the far end of the Mediterranean ... As a lifetime gatherer-upper and carrier of other people's left-behind equipment, I'd be comforted to think he might have been tempted (at least) to say, 'Well, he can darn well freeze!' He'd have brought the stuff along anyway, though; you always do.

There was another offhand instruction in Paul's letter, 'Get Mark and bring him with you ...' Reading the Acts of the Apostles and the letters of Paul, I am always intrigued at how matter-of-factly this kind of instruction is tossed off. Paul was in Rome, both Timothy and Mark seem to have been somewhere in Asia Minor (and not necessarily in the same place). Troas, where the cloak and the books were awaiting transport, was a port town on the coast of what is now Turkey. No problem: 'Bring the cloak', 'get Mark'. They didn't have jet planes in those days, but the early missionaries, like those of today, were expected to be mobile. The overall job they faced was so vast that small practical problems like *getting there* or dealing with excess baggage seemed trivial by comparison, to be dealt with as they came up with no disproportionate fuss.

When Paul scribbles a paragraph of news to Timothy, it is mostly about people being shuttled around ... Luke is here with me, Demas is gone off to Thessalonica, Crescens to Galatia, Titus to Dalmatia. I've sent Tychicus to Ephesus. Erastus is in Corinth. Trophimus is sick, and I had to leave him in Miletus. Timothy knew the places and the people. He'd see the logic behind each appointment without any further information. Also, he'd know who to write to if his own left-behinds needed to be forwarded! Someone should do a study on the similarity between missionaries' letters then and now.

Even the angels knew the code. The one that appeared to the centurion Cornelius instructed him to 'send men to Joppa and fetch hither Peter'. It was two days' walk to Joppa and two days back. No one bothered to ask whether Peter would be willing to come. Cornelius was not a Jew and he was not a Christian, so I suppose you'd have to say he was a pagan. He didn't know Peter and Peter didn't know him. But Peter was under orders now to bring the gospel to the pagans as well as to the Jews. When he accepted the orders, he accepted also the long tramp in the sun, the blistered feet, the uncertain meals, the reorganisation of all his plans. He accepted to be always available, and always to be ready to move – anywhere – at short notice. Whether he realised it or not, he was at the very beginning of what we call *missions*.

Some things about *missions* do not change very much. Suiting your own convenience, for instance, is still not a matter of high priority.

Why not be a missionary?

The necessary average

(October 1979)

Back at Easter I got a letter from Pope John Paul II. Every other priest in the world got the same letter. There was nothing very private about it, and you are free to read it if you want to. It would be a useful thing to do, especially if you are thinking of being a priest yourself. And if you're not, it might start you thinking in that direction, because John Paul II sets a very high value on his own priesthood. He also sets very high standards for his living of it. And for my living of mine, too.

He talks, in the letter, about the kind of priest people need. 'The only priest who will always prove necessary to people,' he writes, 'is the priest who is conscious of the full meaning of his priesthood,
>the priest who believes profoundly,
>who professes his faith with courage,
>who prays fervently,
>who teaches with deep conviction,
>who serves,
>who puts into practice in his own life the
>programmes of the Beatitudes,
>who knows how to love disinterestedly,
>who is close to everyone, and especially to
>those who are most in need ...'

'Well, that's telling them!' you'll say. And indeed it is. But there's nothing new in it, you must know; we've been told exactly the same thing right through the seminary, and many and many a time since. We don't have any doubt about it. It helps, though, when we hear the Pope saying it again in this direct kind of way.

I've seen a comment on the quotation, written by a layman, in an American Catholic newspaper. 'Message for priests hits the spot,' his headline read, but what he said underneath wasn't quite what I expected. The bit of the letter quoted above impressed him, he said, *for two reasons: 'First, the Pope is right,* this *is the kind of priest the people want, but second, because this is exactly the kind of priest we do have in the service of Christ ...'*

A pretty large claim, you may say, but let's hear him out. 'We hear so much about dissenting priests who are leaving the min-

THE NECESSARY AVERAGE

istry of the Church that we start thinking that this minority of priests is almost representative of the priesthood. And this isn't true. The great majority of priests are men who are the kind of priests Pope John Paul described or, because we are all always striving for greater perfection, priests trying to be the kind of priests Pope John Paul described.' (Dale Francis in *The Chicago Catholic*, May 4, 1979)

I'd go along with that *trying to,* at least as far as my own personal acquaintance with priests entitles me to make a judgment. I've been trying to estimate how many priests I know reasonably well. Several hundred, maybe as many as two thousand, and they are all over the world, and they come in all age groups and in all the colours there are. You ask me how many of them don't want to be, or aren't trying to be, something like John Paul II calls for; and I have to tell you I don't know of even one; if I did know of one, I'd have to conclude he was out of his mind. On the other hand, a great many of them do seem to me to match the Pope's description pretty exactly.

It's really a matter of what John Paul II calls *keeping one's word to Christ*. The priests I know tend to be quite serious about this.

Why not be a missionary?

Love constructs

(March 1980)

A boy on my mind. Seventeen going on eighteen. An evening last August he was swimming with friends in light surf in a warm sea. A big roller coming, he got all the purchase he could from the shifting sand underfoot to dive powerfully into the breaking crest of it. And then, in one terrible moment, he knew he was going to drown, there in the shallow water, with the big wave already spent. Some kind of freaky accident; he had smashed his third and fourth vertebrae in that dive. No pain – yet, just that he was paralysed totally, unable to move even a finger. At seventeen, with the blue sky over him, he knew he was going to die.

In fact, he did not die; when they realised he wasn't fooling they pulled him out, not a second too soon. Got him to hospital, not comprehending, only half believing. He's been moved to another hospital since. Six, seven months, an eternity. He can move three fingers, just a little, now. Will he make further improvement? The doctors are not saying.

A girl on my mind. Joyous, vibrant, and twenty-three. That was three months ago. Three months ago minus one day she felt ill. One week ago, everyone knew she had perhaps ten days to live. All *she* knew was one single pervading enormous pain. And one single pervading enormous joy. In those three months she discovered Christ. He is the love of her life. Take me, or cure me, is her prayer. What you want is what I want.

Another boy. Steadfast, tranquil, perfectly adjusted to the fact that he somehow got an advanced case of lung cancer without ever smoking, and the end of the road plainly in sight.

And *why?* you ask. They are so young. They are so good. Why are they stricken in such awful ways? What kind of sense does it make, youngsters of their calibre out of the race like this? What marvels they might have wrought in the world …

Correction: what marvels they *have* wrought, what mighty things they continually accomplish in the world! You must be clear: these stricken young people are not out of the race. They are in a different *kind* of race. Often, it seems that because the going is so much tougher there it is only those who excel

LOVE CONSTRUCTS

supremely that qualify to take part in it. The real greats. It is all tied in somehow with the *great* of all time, who was fixed, hands and feet, totally helpless and immobilised, at the moment when he broke down all barriers for us and opened all doors.

That boy with the smashed vertebrae would tell you that his moment of death under the blue August sky taught him that every moment of his reprieve has to be *lived* intensely. He may never move more than those three fingers, but he fills his days moving mountains for the rest of us.

The joyous girl in her enormous pain beams the power of her enormous joyous love on the world's hatreds and resentments. 'Love constructs,' Pope John Paul II declares, 'only love constructs.' She is too busy building to need your pity. And the steadfast boy with the lung cancer is doing more than you know to resolve your personal daily puzzlements. Don't pity him, he's stronger perhaps than you.

The real question is, what are *you* doing? You with the youth, the health? You with no handicap? And what am I doing? Slower now because older, but still with the health, no handicap? What do we fill our days with, our moments? We who are *in the race,* how intensely do *we* live? Shall we, we who have a choice – shall we henceforth construct?

Why not be a missionary?

Giving the treatment

(June/July 1980)

We're driving down this jammed street, inch by inch, five deep on the carriageway, and the odd motorcycle taking to the footpath. It is the morning rush hour. Whatever has happened up ahead, maybe an accident, a roadsquad setting up to do a repair job, a traffic light gone crazy, or maybe the traffic police gone on strike, we're all certainly going to be good and late for work. You might think our common difficulty would make brothers of us all, but mild men become tigers in traffic, and in fact we don't seem to like one another very much. No smiles, no cordial salutes from one vehicle to another, just take every advantage you can, and woe betide the weak.

Here's one weak one now, wanting to insert his brand new car into the line out of a side street, but not daring to push. He's been waiting there for ten minutes. The line begins to move again. I catch his appealing eye, ignore the hornblast behind, and beckon him forward. He waves fervent thanks, lets out his clutch too fast – and stalls. Now he's flustered and does everything wrong and the horns blast furiously back along the line. At last he gets things under control and takes his place in front of me gratefully. Too gratefully, I think, as he turns right round to smile and bow and wave to me. A small courtesy shouldn't have to be such a big deal. We're Christians, aren't we?

Inching along, I reflect about this. People asked Christ more than once – good men asked him, and bad men asked him – what was the greatest and the first commandment. He always gave the same answer. Love the Lord your God: that is the first commandment. And the second is like unto this: love your neighbour as yourself. He put it another way: always treat others as you would like them to treat you. Always. Always. Yes, we are Christians, and that is what a Christian must do.

Some of us, maybe, are born kind, thoughtful, tactful, unselfish and loving. Most of us aren't, and we have to work on it! We are not going to treat others as we'd like them to treat us unless we make a habit of putting ourselves in their shoes. If I were that man whose cattle all died, if I were that mother with the handicapped child, if I were that timid lady in the lonely bedsitter, or that hopeful salesman at the door, or that intoxicated man lying by the roadside ... If I were that neighbour in hospital, that third-rate singer on the stage, that disgraced one trying to lift his head once more in the community ... how would I want them to treat me? If I were starving, or desperate, or even just painfully shy. If I needed encouragement, understanding, sympathy – or congratulation? I shouldn't have far to look, with Christ's people all around me. Should I?

If I had no idea why I was born, or what life was really about, or what (if anything) happened afterwards, I'd like someone to tell me.

If I had never heard that my creator loves me, loves me now, has loved me always, and wants me with him forever in his blissful home of many mansions, I'd surely want to be told. If I did not know he'd sent his only Son to share my lot, if I did not know he died for me, and rose from the dead and lifted me up with him, and made sense of the things I suffer, and made the way clear before me ... If I did not know this, and if there were hundreds of millions of fortunate people within reach of me who did know it ... well, I'd have thought they might have gone to the trouble of telling me.

I'd have told *them* if the positions had been reversed. Wouldn't I?

> Why not be a missionary?

Raise a shout

(March 1981)

What do we do? Well, often enough we just moan about what other people don't do. The press of the world is full of our *belly-aching* about the inequalities in society. We'll carry a banner anywhere, join in any protest: against world hunger, social injustice, the widening gap between rich and poor, colour discrimination, racism – you name it. But there is too much *they*, too little *we*, hardly any *I*, in a lot of this demonstration we do.

When will it strike us that we are the real rich, the real privileged? Who'll explode it into our consciousness that we are hoarding, mindlessly, a treasure which is inexhaustible? There is plenty for everyone – and yet we behave as though we were content that there should be two billion people who have nothing – while we have all! We claim, don't we – we boast we're Christians! We ought to know that man's first need is for the *kingdom* of God and his justice. We have Christ's word for it that all the rest will be added.

We ought to know that man does not live on bread alone; that his deepest hunger is for the word of God. But will we give him the word of God? Will we invite him into our privileged community? Pressingly? As though we really meant it? Or are we going to just go on playing down the very thing that matters most, accepting the world's criterion of the meaning of true charity?

Perhaps the devil has a new line. Is it he who is suggesting to Christians that it is somehow insensitive or indelicate to preach the gospel to hungry people until after they've been fed? What a pity Christ didn't know! He gave them the word first and fed them later.

It doesn't hurt us a bit – or help anyone else very much – if we look upon the deprivations of the underprivileged and make the fashionable but dubious general confession that *we are all guilty*. Corporate guilt is easy enough to live with. But if God's *chosen race* hoards his saving gospel, how can it escape the guilt of the worst kind of racism? If God's *people set apart* grudge to reach out welcoming hands to all mankind, are they not guilty of a strange spiritual *apartheid?* Where shall we look, you and I, for pardon, if we transform Christ's *society of hope* into a closed shop?

There are six hundred million of us. We ought to be able to raise a shout that all the world can hear! But listen carefully and you'll hear something near enough to *the sound of silence*.

You could call us, like Paul, *ambassadors in chains* – but our chains are of our own making. Fashionable chains that the current whimsy of the world might approve, but that does no honour to Christians – or to Christ.

No one puts a gag in our mouths. Most of us are entirely free to tell the world what we know. Maybe we need to have an honest look at ourselves. Maybe we should say Paul's prayer: 'that utterance may be given me in opening my mouth boldly to proclaim the mystery of the gospel ... that I may declare it boldly, as I ought to speak.'

Why not be a missionary?

Breaking bread

(May 1981)

I am not very good at faces, but I remember this man's face so clearly that if I were an artist I could draw it for you in faithful detail. I know I should feel a great deal worse about my sins than I do about what I did to this man in the year 1957, through no fault of my own, but truthfully this has caused me more enduring remorse than if it had been a sin.

The thing was so elementary that nobody had thought of telling me about it. So when I went for a walk and wandered into this man's compound by accident and was welcomed by him with what would have roughly corresponded to a twenty-one gun salute – I didn't know how to respond.

He was a noble figure of an old man with wrinkles and a grey stubble of beard and dancing eyes. First he shook my hand many times uttering little cries of delight. Then he went and found something in a basket by his house. Suddenly solemn, he held this object up for inspection. It looked like a large flattish purple chestnut; it was in fact a kola nut. He licked this along its length and made a little drama of presenting it to me. And I didn't know what to do! His look changed from expectancy to bewilderment as I inspected his offering, thanked him warmly – and put it in my pocket. I knew something was wrong, but I didn't know what …

It embarrasses me even to think of it. I now know, of course, that the man was offering me symbolic hospitality. He licked the kola to show me it was safe to eat, that is, not poisoned. I should immediately have broken the nut in two, given one portion back to him and put the other in my mouth. Then we would have eaten together. A little meal to be eaten in friendship and trust. A pledge that this man would never do me wrong, nor I him. We could have been friends for life. The best I can hope is that he gave me a fool's pardon.

I wonder if the happiest passages in the gospel are not those which tell of food and drink. Christ thirsty outside the Samaritan town asking the woman for a drink from her jar. Christ hosting the multitudes (and eating with them surely) when he multiplied the loaves and fishes. Christ a guest in the friendly house of Lazarus. Presiding tenderly at the Last Supper. Breaking bread in Emmaus with the two disciples. Eating the piece of fish in the Upper Room to prove he was real. Roasting fish for the apostles' breakfast by the Sea of Galilee?

These scribes and pharisees were on to something important when they complained that he made a habit of eating with publicans and sinners, but they missed its real significance. I don't know why it is, but there are few surer ways to win a man's friendship than to let him make you his guest. To eat and drink what he puts before you and let him see that you enjoy it. To share what you've got with him if you are the one with the food. Most of all, as the old man with the kola knew very well, to eat – together. Call it the *communion* part. Christ knew about this. (I think if *we* grasped it a little better, our trips to Mass would do a lot more for us; but that's another question.)

The faces I remember longest from among the people I met only once in my life are the old man with the kola in 1957, the two-bit politician with the disabled Mercedes who was glad to share my sandwiches and coffee when I gave him a lift one black, wet night on a forest road, the Fulani herdsman who did me a similar honour once on a northern plateau, and a woman *with a name in the town* (as one bible translation delicately puts it) who saw me drenched and mud-spattered after a difficult river crossing and offered me a drink to warm me from a black bottle of moonshine, and had concern in her eyes. All four are from years ago, but they will always be high on the list of friends that I pray for. Next time we eat together, I hope, it will be in a kingdom, with all the others there, and God sitting down with us.

Why not be a missionary?

Why not be a missionary?

(March 1982)

'Midnight Greenwich Mean Time, BBC World Service, the News, read by ...' I'll never know who the newsreader was, because I fell asleep at that point. No reflection, let me say, on a superb radio service which has kept me at least literate on world events for more than half a lifetime. When I woke up, it was nearly dawn, the radio was still going, and somebody was talking about a Bizet symphony composed for a medium-sized orchestra without trombones. I felt sorry about the trombones (and about my batteries), but cheered myself sleepily with the thought that there would still be strings, the woodwinds, the drums and, above all, the dramatic figure away at the back with the great brass cymbals in his outflung hands, awaiting his moment, and heaven help him if he mistimes that marvellous clash. I got out of bed wondering if cymbals players have a recurring nightmare about this. That was before I was awake enough to recall my own current nightmare ...

I'm supposed to do something *special* for this Golden Jubilee Special. It is expected to be about this *Why not be a missionary?* feature itself (call it a nightmare about a recurring nightmare, if you like) ... 'how it started, how it's been continued, its aim, what success it's had, *etc.*'

Let's say it started out of a compulsion and continued out of conviction, and continues to continue because a series of editors continues to hound me. It would be nice to be able to say I have been compelled by popular demand, but it wouldn't be true. I get fan mail about once in five years; last year *the letter* came from a nun in Malawi who claimed she used the piece for her spiritual reading; in 1976 a priest wrote from England to tell me he keeps a stack of these pieces by his bedside and reads one before he goes to sleep. Well, evidently I've not been *aiming* at nuns or priests, though if something I say gets to them I'm happy about it, of course. I've been aiming, maybe you remember, at John Smith, the common denominator among boys or men who might have, or develop, a vocation to be a missionary priest. John Smith is a type that doesn't smother you with *feedback,* so in the thirty years the feature has been going out there have been indications maybe five or six times that it has at least put a thought in somebody's head.

It began when I was fresh from my first spell in Africa. It had been a four-year tour and I had been switched so many times from one place to another, and had seen so many others similarly switched, that I was conscious that the missions were understaffed. The work was booming, and even one man going sick or taking leave created a veritable crisis. People were clamouring at the doors – for sacraments, schools, instruction, comfort, counsel. It was marvellous, and it was devastating; giving the very best we could, we were still only skimming the surface. The best image was the scriptural one, the ripe harvest with far too few reapers. So the writing began out of compulsion.

The first thing I learned in Africa was that I knew nothing about it. Long afterwards, someone discovered a thing called *cultural shock*. I suppose we all experienced it, without a neat name for it. In our years of training, we had been given as much as experienced missionaries could give us in the way of information, but it was by doing and by experiencing that we really learned about being a missionary.

That is why I say the *Why not be a missionary?* feature continued out of a conviction. The conviction was that you could not share the experience of being a priest, or of being a missionary, with anyone in one catch-all piece of writing. The best you could do was to give it in small pieces, one aspect at a time, one angle, one aspect. Also, people become missionaries for a lot of different reasons, even if the one main reason is a constant, and any particular aspect might provide the stimulant that could set a particular individual on his way. That's a conviction that keeps you going; and somehow the arguments don't seem to run out.

This Golden Jubilee of the Society provides just one more (for pity's sake, let's not use all the space reminiscing!). Fifty years is a fairly long time in a man's life, you'd agree? Well now, there are people who have been all that time with the Society, doing an active missionary job. Come down the year-scale, to the forties and thirties and twenties; there are many others at every point, out of sight in the far places, still doing what they set out to do when still in their teens. Nothing spectacular, you know, just digging in the faith, just taking pastoral care of the new Christian generations, just happily burning out their lives in an enterprise they took on in youth. Just being missionary priests, and staying with it, at any cost. It costs plenty, but it is still the only thing they want to do; they are very sure of that.

Then the younger ones: they keep coming, you see, in spite of all the counter attractions, they mesh into the team, bringing it new life, new ideas, new (sometimes better) methods. They know they're needed, they assume they're welcome, and they're going to do what they came to do anyway. They are the future. They and – yes, indeed yes – those other younger ones, the John Smiths, who haven't yet committed themselves but who could possibly be persuaded.

For maybe one of those unknowns the right word at the right time just might make the small difference that tips the scale. That's why I have a fellow-feeling with the cymbals player. Does he sometimes pray, I wonder, that he may not miss the moment? I know I do. If you, faithful reader, were to add a prayer of your own, there would be no objection.

Doing it my way

(November 1982)

The praying part of the morning is routine, maybe too routine, and it is finished by seven forty-five and then there's a slot for coffee. The first job of the working day is a meeting sharp at eight-thirty. Busy people will be waiting, ten minutes' drive away, for the raw material I carry in a folder under my arm. I've been through the stuff in the night watches. I am well prepared and easy. It is only eight o'clock, so I am comfortable for time. Too comfortable! I push in the ignition key and turn it and – tkkk! – the starter jams. No sweat, I know what to do. I rock the car violently. No good. I search for a grip and rock it the other way, back and forward with the gear in; no good. By now, I am sweaty and dirty. I know another trick, however. Find a log of wood and hammer it on the starting motor. I hammer. The thing stays jammed. My half hour has slipped away.

Another ten minutes finding a mechanic. He comes with a helper, not willingly. I will demonstrate the problem. I turn the ignition key. Everything works. The engine starts instantly. I am left looking foolish. The rest of the day follows the same pattern. I never really get it back on the rails. A lot of my days are like that. They don't go the way I've planned them. It is probably good for my character, but it hardly leaves things tidy. Night prayer is routine. I bring the whole mess to God, grinning apologetically (he knows me by now), and hope he will make something useful out of it in spite of all.

It isn't just the days; the weeks and years are like that, too. I start something that I reckon should take six months to round off neatly. Two years and ten starts later, I still have not got it off the ground. But *why?* Partly me, I suppose, and my limitations; but other things, people, circumstances I cannot control, are part of the reason also. Mainly, I think, God wants it done (*if* he wants it done) – *his* way, in the time *he* decides. Should I quarrel with that?

There is a piece in the Old Testament that I like very much, where King David gets the idea that he should build a grand house for God. 'But that same night the word of the Lord came to Nathan: "Go and tell my servant David" …' Tell him what?

No house, forget it! 'I will raise up your offspring after you, who shall come forth from your body, and I will establish his kingdom. *He* shall build a house for my name, and I will establish the throne of his kingdom for ever ...' *For ever* is a long time, and I think David sensed that this prophecy was looking a long way beyond his son Solomon and the temple *he* would one day build. He certainly knew that this was very big stuff indeed; that much is evident from the prayer he said immediately afterwards when he 'went in and sat before the Lord'.

I do not have Nathan around to bring me divine revelations when I'm planning something that seems important and the starter jams. Whenever there is a foul-up, I know it is probably because *I did it my way*; the only way I knew, to be sure, but not necessarily the best way, or God's way. But then, God could have put somebody else in my place, and he didn't.

When David was at one of his low points and running for his life, he asked the priest in Hebron for the loan of a weapon to defend himself. He was told that the only weapon in the house was the sword with which he himself had killed Goliath, a sort of museum piece. And David said eagerly, 'Give it to me, there is no other sword like that!' The sight of it reassured him. He was still God's warrior.

And I am still a missionary, I tell myself sometimes when I strike a low. That has not changed since the day it began, despite all my bungling, past, present, and to come. The original purpose is firm, even if its execution leaves practically everything to be desired! And I think how David went in and sat before the Lord and said, 'Who am I, O Lord God, and what is my house, that thou hast brought me this far ...?'

Why not be a missionary?

Holding hands

(January/February 1983)

Every day the routine was the same, every day for six or seven years. Early in the morning the farmer carried a sack of potatoes into his kitchen and dumped it near the door. All through the day his wife gave away the potatoes, one by one. Often, halfway through the day the sack was empty, and the farmer replaced it with a full one. There was no end to the procession of the hungry. None of them got much, but none went away empty-handed. Each one got a potato. One potato.

It was in the thirties, along the Dutch/German border, when hundreds of men with no job and nothing to eat roamed the country asking for food. One potato was not much of a meal, but it was a ration that could be depended upon at that farmer's house. And there you have the story of one plain countryman's practical charity. Four hundred sacks of potatoes in a year, when you think of it, was no small gift.

It happens I know one of that farmer's sons. It happens he spends his life roaming the world finding practical ways to feed the world's hungry. Just a coincidence, you say? You could be right. All I am saying is that when this man was a little boy he was often in his parents' kitchen. He saw what went on there.

Another story, this one from Umbria in middle Italy. Two little girls walking five kilometres from school on winter evenings. Oftentimes when they reached home their mother met them with a hug, an apology – and an apple: 'I'm sorry, girls, you will have to do with this; a poor man called and I gave him your dinner. He was very hungry.'

I know a lady in her fifties, a breezy, good-hearted person with a lot of friends. Five years ago she suddenly disappeared from sight. She gave up her job, her flat, her social life, her freedom of movement, even her independence, to move in with a neurotic old woman she heard of who was going out of her mind with loneliness and fear. She is still with her, tied to her, you might almost say, hand and foot. 'Sometimes,' she explains, 'you have to face it that you are a Christian and ask yourself what that means.' Now it happens this lady was one of the little girls whose mother used to give away their dinner. Again, this is perhaps no more than a coincidence …

But it does suggest a reflection for New Year. Where do Christians come from, real ones, the sort who are serious about the greatest and the first commandment and about the second which is like unto it? They come generally from families where love is liberally mixed into the daily diet, with enough left over to give to the neighbours.

And where does that leave your family?

It leaves it at the beginning of a New Year and at the beginning of the future. At a point of decision; we shuffle along as we always have, *or* we set out *now* at least, all of us together and really in earnest, to cure what is wrong with the world.

The place to start, and we know it, is right here at home on our own hearthstone. Love is something one has to work at, with many failures. Love is something to be learned, by imperfect parents and imperfect children both, and even the littlest one can help with the lesson, and the oldest can be in need of instruction. Love is made of listening, of bending down to say I'm sorry, of forgiving readily, of biting words back when the urge is to nag, of starting a conversation to break a hostile silence, of respecting sensitivities, heading off quarrels, praising generously, showing appreciation, peacemaking. Love is praying together, knowing we are a family. Love is gathering around the hurt one. Love is doing without things together so that someone in need may be given a little. Love is being really genuinely a Christian, or a family of Christians.

Oh, and – shall I tell you where missionaries come from, or do you prefer to tell me?

Why not be a missionary?

'Doesn't the thought of dying terrify you?'

(June/July 1983)

My father's generation, I recall, paid a large amount of attention to the formalities of dying and getting buried. Wakes and funerals provided quite significant – if not to say welcome! – breaks in the routine of their lives, and they remembered the details of them for ages afterwards, as well as the exact dates of countless anniversaries. The first thing they went for on the newspaper was the list of deaths, and we brash young ones used to accuse them jokingly of suffering a certain disappointment if it did not contain the name of some acquaintance. They liked to be first with the news when someone died, and the sad event provided matter for conversation for several days. Except that ... for them death did not seem to be a *sad event*. They felt easy with it. It was a normal and natural part of living and it happened all the time. Also, their frequent ritual references to the probable imminence of their own deaths was, I felt, something of an act. They really expected to live to a ripe old age and eventually to die (and how they loved these phrases!) full of years and *fortified by the rites of holy Church*. And it was remarkable, in the event, how many of them actually did.

I got to remembering all this recently when a wonderfully good mother of a family telephoned me to say she had a very bad dose of bronchial pneumonia and was ordered to stay in bed for a month. She added that she was feeling dreadful and was terrified that she might die. She asked me: 'Doesn't the thought of dying terrify you?'

The question was unexpected, and I found I needed a minute or two to think before I could be sure I knew how to answer it sincerely. I found myself saying, 'No, I don't think so. I won't say I want to hurry the moment; it is likely to be uncomfortable, maybe painful; but certainly not terrifying.' Not one of the people I have seen dying has died in anything like terror. And, anyway, you make a half decent effort at Christian living and there is something you can absolutely depend on; the help or courage or comfort you need will be there when you need it. When you know that you don't try to cross any bridges before you need them, you know you can cross them with dignity when the time comes. It is one of the bonuses.

As for what comes afterwards, I think again of my father's generation. They talked a lot about the pains of purgatory and kept us on our knees many a night praying for friends who might be delayed there. But it was perfectly clear that they had a powerful curiosity about that *place or state* of purification, and they were so sure of God's love and mercy that the thought of it did not bother them one bit! And as to hell? ... that is a reality, to be sure, but only for someone who has stamped out the last spark of love in his soul.

Am I being too *comfortable* about all this? A few weeks ago, and a long way from here, Brother Denis, one of my dearest friends, died. Offering Mass for him when the news reached me, I was persistently distracted by one recollection: how when I had stayed a night with him in Mallow once, on my way to an early morning appointment in Cork city centre, he had insisted on leading me all the way by little quiet roads he knew so that I shouldn't get stuck in the rush-hour traffic. A small journey at the beginning of his day's work, and he thought nothing of it. But it was one of the million kindnesses of which his life was made; and if I was remembering it, there was no danger God was going to forget!

No less than three times in the past couple of years, one or other of my missionary colleagues in different parts of the world finished their day's tasks and sat down with their breviaries for a bit of quiet prayer – and just quietly died there alone. With their day's work done.

Very recently Seán Deegan, who started secondary school with me and went through Kiltegan with me and spent all the years of his priesthood as a missionary and pastor in Africa, came in from out-station confessions, reeling with fever and joking in his good-humoured way about the fuss his concerned household was making about it. Seán died without fuss on the way to hospital. No terror there. Just a lot of reassurance for us who will go on missing him.

Why not be a missionary?

Works and pomps

(March 1984)

I have been sitting for minutes past looking at a picture of Michael the Archangel and testing myself to see if I can still recite the prayer to him that was always said after Mass up to about the end of the fifties. It was a tough, unrelenting sort of prayer in which we asked the Archangel to *defend us in the day of battle* and urged him to *thrust Satan down to hell, and with him the other wicked spirits who wander through the world for the ruin of souls.*

I remember that when I was growing up I enjoyed the martial rhythm of that prayer, but at the same time I had a sneaking sympathy for the fallen angels and wondered if perhaps we were not being too severe on them. I suppose I had not yet seen much evil and therefore was not over-conscious of the malevolence of the powers of hell. Or maybe I recognised even then that I had a few faults and failings myself, and did not feel that I had any right to throw stones – even at the devils.

None of these reservations remain. I find I can say the prayer now with enthusiasm and conviction. I look at Guido Reni's old picture of Michael looping a chain around the evil one and I say, *Bravo!* Bind him fast, Archangel, because everywhere I look today I see the evidence of his activity. Thrust him down to hell with all his works and pomps, because he has had his way with the sons of men for far too long, and they, the fools, have been too willing to play his games with him.

The angel in the picture is strong and powerful, with muscles rippling beneath the skintight heavenly armour. He rests a foot on the head of the ugly cringing evil one, and his sword is pointed downwards at him menacingly. But there is no anger on his face; just a great sureness and an unemotional distaste. You see that good will have no truck with evil, and that good has no doubt of its power to conquer it. Good has no fear of evil, but certainly does not propose to let it get an advantage.

I look beyond the picture to the headlines on the day's paper. Divisions among men. Hatred, revenge, reprisal, oppression, murder, violence, kidnapping, robbery, drug-pushing, greed, idleness, pride, lust, despair, starvation, fear, terror. Yes, the evil is there, and the powers of evil are energetic in promoting it.

But there is the other side, and I know it, and you know it. Most of the people I know and you know are not murderers or drug-pushers or kidnappers or terrorists or bandits. Neither are they especially greedy or ruthless or without pity or seething with hate. Most people I know – and most you know, surely – are consistently trying to be good. Many, in fact, are already heroically good, selfless, loving, caring and generous.

It often seems to me that the devil is busiest when he is worried. He is most vicious whenever truth and love and goodness look like gaining the upper hand. This makes me very optimistic about the times we are living in. He has been striking out madly for the past few years and always going for the jugular: corrupt the youth, degrade the priesthood, sabotage the consecrated life, disrupt the family, downgrade chastity, stimulate greed, make a mockery of honest dealing, keep people at each other's throats, sow distrust, trample the weak, starve the poor, destroy the unborn, distort the news, suborn the media ...

It is all old stuff, of course, fancied up to look like the new enlightenment. We can fall for it. We can go along with it and give him an easy victory. *But we need not*. We are free to do right. Not all the powers of hell can rob us of that. We are free, in fact, to take an offensive of our own, to leave all things and follow Christ to the ends of the earth with a word of truth and love and peace. Very many still do!

Why not be a missionary?

Wise old hard sayings

(May 1984)

The primary school readers on which my generation cut its literary teeth were packed with ancient wisdom, maxims and proverbs so self-evidently unassailable that we sometimes used them even to settle our fights. There were stitches in time that saved nine, rolling stones that gathered no moss, early birds catching early worms, young heads that could not be put on old shoulders, birds of a feather that flocked together, and clever humans that got rich because they were early to bed and early to rise (a thing we found specially obnoxious).

One proverb that provoked much sardonic comment in our suffering ranks came from our Irish book. It said: *mol an óige agus tiocfaidh sí* – praise the young and they will make progress. Praise in our experience was about as rare as gold ingots. Mostly, what progress we made was the result of wholesome fear, and whatever excellence we eventually attained is probably attributable to an unwritten pedagogical principle that if you tell them often enough what stupid, bone lazy, wicked, lying, good-for-nothing misfits they are, their natural cussedness will force them to prove to you that they are nothing of the kind. Just to put you in the wrong.

We live in changed times. The principle now seems to be that if you tell them they are marvellous, they will break a leg trying to prove to you how right you are. (Was it St Francis de Sales that said a spoonful of honey could accomplish more than a barrel of vinegar?) '*Carissimi,*' (dearest ones) says Pope John Paul to a mob of bright-faced youngsters, 'you are the hope, the joy, the vitality, of every society, civil and ecclesiastical.' True, of course. But in the back of my mind I hear my venerated teachers of long ago commenting: 'Easy *for* them! Joy and vitality are God's free gifts to youth, they didn't have to lift a finger to earn them. And hope – well, hope is something that by its nature has yet to be fulfilled!' (They never called us *carissimi,* by the way. We'd have dropped down dead.)

Certainly they allowed themselves no rosy-tinted illusions about youth, those stern teachers of the past. They knew that original sin was alive and well in the young, as in every other age group (give an inch and they'll take an ell) and that it had to be firmly curbed if later disasters were to be averted (spare the rod and spoil the child). But in their unbending way they loved their reluctant charges very deeply (loving is as loving does); they recognised in the young the hope of a future and spared no pains to see that the hope was realised. Yes, but far-off hills are green, they reminded themselves, and there is many a slip between the cup and the lip – so they made timely provision to offset the assaults of human weakness, fecklessness and indolence.

They did it with the ten commandments of God, the six commandments of the Church, the gifts and fruits of the Holy Ghost, the sacraments, the cardinal virtues, the fear of hell, the fear of losing heaven, and the unthinkable horror of being separated from God. They did it with fasting, abstinence and everything they could find in the penny catechism, the temperance catechism, the bible history and the four gospels. They did it with practical lessons in prayer. They did it by the inflexible example of their own poured-out splendid lives.

What they taught was a lived (and therefore liveable) Christianity, without sugar-coating, thinning-down, evasion or apology. It included all the tenderness, and it left out none of the hard sayings. It suppressed none of the promises, did no glossing over of the vital requirements to love God and neighbour – and left Christ's cross standing starkly over everything else in the place of greatest prominence. For without that, what could we ever know about love, how could we ever cope with hardship, whence could we draw courage or resolution to learn unselfishness and step daily in Christ's footprints?

There was no proverb in the primary school reader to buttress that last piece, except perhaps *easy come easy go,* or *eaten bread soon forgotten,* but there is no law saying we cannot make one up. So, pick freely from the following: 'Crossless Christianity, gutless Christian'; 'Health wealth hurt hate, – sugar-coated Christian's fate'. Or better still, listen to Paul the missionary: 'When I came to you, brethren, I did not come with lofty words or wisdom. For I decided to know nothing among you except Jesus Christ and him crucified.'

Why not be a missionary?

Measuring up

(July/August 1985)

I've read somewhere that in Japanese factories they often have a room equipped with mansized punchbags. If you're feeling mad with the boss, or the shop steward, or the wife, or a fellow worker, you are free to go and beat the daylights out of one of these dummies, pretending to yourself that it is the person you are mad with. So you get it out of your system and return well-satisfied to your bench or assembly line to turn out more Mitsubishis or whatever. A civilised idea indeed: nobody gets hurt, violence is dissipated harmlessly, and production is only momentarily interrupted.

They were probably not so much concerned about production back in the old scriptural days as they were with seeing the offender soundly punished. Beating up a punchbag wouldn't have satisfied them. They had this unpleasant habit of stoning people. Now, as a method of execution stoning was probably no worse than any other. It distributed the responsibility by allowing active community participation, it was economical (stones were plentiful), and it was effective – well, usually. Questions, however, arise in the mind: Were there rules you had to keep? Did you, for instance, have to throw from a certain distance? Did the interested party get a sporting chance (like the hare at a coursing match)? Were there champion stoners in every community? Was there applause when the marksmanship was particularly good? Or, were spectators allowed?

But of course we know they were; did not Paul take care of the garments of the worthies who stoned Stephen? And he was no neutral either. Paul, in fact, would be something of an authority on stoning; he saw it, you might say, from both ends. There was, you will recall, that memorable day in Lystra when he himself was stoned, and thrown out of the city, and left for dead. One case, anyway, where stoning as a method of execution proved less than one hundred per cent efficient. Or maybe there was a little miracle, I don't know. All we're told is that when his disciples gathered round him, he rose up and entered the city. And the very next day (stiff and sore, you may be sure), he left for Derbe, another town down the road a bit. Just a day's-walking away!

They say he spent maybe five years in Derbe that time, working as a journeyman tent-maker during the day, instructing his new Christians whenever he had a chance, and very carefully building up one of the first little communities of Gentile Christians. Hard work, and he wasn't in the best of health, but he put everything he knew into that Church at Derbe. It was his first real *mission* and it was very special to him ever afterwards, as any modern day missionary will easily understand. They would have plucked out their eyes for him, he tells them years later. He expected the best from them always, and he knew them well enough to write them his strongest abuse when they failed to measure up. Abuse with the love showing through.

It was not all that far from Derbe to Paul's home town, Tarsus. (Well, maybe ten days' hard walking through some of the most terrifying mountain passes in the world.) Paul could have done with a holiday at home after these five demanding years. But he turned his face to the north, and his back towards Tarsus. Back he went to Lystra, where they had stoned him. Back to Iconium after that, which he had left one jump ahead of the posse on his last visit. Back to Antioch in Pisidia to spend time with the folk there whom he had had to leave only partially instructed. Back to Perga on the coast to found the Church he had not had time to found first time through. All the way back on his own tracks he went, however doubtful might his welcome be, however likely might be a new stoning episode. A stubborn, driven, fearless man, this apostle Paul, with one priority uppermost in his mind … and certain that this was the one thing he wanted to achieve with his life.

Up against this commitment and conviction any modern missionary is free to measure his own, and sometimes the conclusion may not be reassuring. Still, and don't you doubt it, there are plenty of missionaries today who measure up. And there's no good reason why there should not be many more.

(For the background to this, the reader is invited to refer to Acts 13 and 14.)

Why not be a missionary?

Six mile high

(November 1985)

Thirty-five thousand feet above the earth on a perfectly clear summer day. There must surely be some simple way of calculating precisely how far I can see from my window-seat in the jet: drop a six mile perpendicular, measure the angle between the top of it and the point at the limit of vision, allow for the earth's curvature, and simply apply the formula, whatever it is ... Child's play for every schoolboy with a calculator, but well beyond my range. I satisfy myself with a guess: let's say a hundred miles, grass, forest, rivers. It looks as if it might be a pleasant place to live. Hardly at all what I should have expected, for that is Siberia down there. Endless miles of smiling summer country, but in five hours I have not seen a single sign of human habitation, nothing I could identify as a house, or a road, or a flock, or a herd. Who says the world is over-populated!

And then, at last, I see a town. It is not very big, and it is very compact and it lies on the bank of a wide river. Something odd about it, but it takes a moment or two to identify what it is. It is two things: the town is all on one bank of the river, there is nothing on the other bank, and there is no bridge. Also, there is no trace of a road into the town; whatever comes or goes evidently has to come or go by the river, but there is no boat in sight. Quite quickly the odd little town passes from beneath me, and I look out once more across my hundred miles of empty summer country, wondering. Several hours later we make a fuelling stop at Moscow, then hurry on across Poland to Frankfurt ... and several years later I find myself still wondering idly about that strangely isolated town in Siberia, and find no answers ...

What is it that I want to know? Well, that's hardly the question. It's a matter of feeling, I think, rather than of knowing. I have no picture of this town's people in my mind. Somehow there are no lines of communication. Kinshasa, for instance, for me is massed friendly lights seen across the Zaire River deep in the night from Brazzaville. Tokyo is sidewalks thronged with hurrying oriental faces, all stamped with western anxiety. It is also a train coming down a street straddling its monorail wall. Sydney is a winged opera house by the water, miles of used car lots, and a kindly taximan who undertakes to post my letters when I have neither stamps nor money. Lagos is multitudes who never become anonymous, pounding surf on a beach with coconut palms, numberless people who find time to help one another. Hong Kong is a scary passage between beautiful hills into an oval of skyscrapers and someone who says good morning to a stranger. New York is people going home with groceries on a Sunday morning in Flushing, and a taximan in Manhattan who earnestly tries to run me down. London is seeing all the streets you've read about, from the top of a bus, and a street sweeper walking half a mile to put you on the right road. Paris is beauty and a lift of the heart and overcharging and a love-hate thing about the French ... and so on.

But this town, nothing. No vibes. No liking or disliking. No picture in the heart. A cluster of houses on the bank of an unknown river, hardly even breaking the monotony of totally empty summer countryside. Neutral, feelingless, featureless. But it has stayed with me for years, and I wanted to talk about it. Maybe that is because I sometimes find myself praying about it. 'You are with me in my comings in and going out. Your eyes roamed Siberia with mine that summer day, and rested on that anonymous town along the fiftieth parallel, and recognised each one of its inhabitants, and had plans for each, and ways to apply your redemption to them that I cannot even begin to guess at. But I want to be a part of it, somehow. And I don't believe they are out of reach ...'

Why not be a missionary?

Read to the end of the story

(May 1986)

It could be the woman's husband was a no-good lout. It could be he battered her, abused the children, squandered his earnings, played around with other women. A good lawyer might have made a reasonably strong case in her defence. But she stood there alone with no one to plead for her. Everyone was an accuser. Nobody had a single word to say in her favour.

Oh, and she was guilty as charged. And she knew it. Guilt was written all over her. The evidence against her was incontestable. Another thing, and she probably knew this too, was that she was man-in-the-middle in a power-struggle between great forces. Bigger issues than her personal delinquencies were at stake. She was expendable.

Anyway, that's how it looked. The only thing left was a plea for clemency. She saw that was hopeless and she didn't try it. Neither did anybody else. So ... it was up to the judge and he didn't have any choices; the sentence was mandatory.

The judge was saying nothing. He was away in a world of his own, bent down, doodling on the sand. When he did speak eventually, his summing-up took her guilt for granted; took for granted also that the mandatory punishment was well merited. But as the last shuffle of departing feet died away and she found herself alone before him, she knew that he had cleverly saved her. She knew that, where he was concerned, she was not expendable.

A beautiful story of divine mercy in John's chapter eight, but it must be read to the end. Christ was gentle and forgiving to the woman who had sinned, but Christ was not sentimental about sin. 'Go,' he said to her, 'and do not sin again.' You've got to note that he calls it by its name, bluntly. For him, there is no euphemism for sin. And this is not the only case in the gospel where he tells the forgiven sinner not to do it again.

If you become a priest, John Smith, in the times we live in, and if you're going to insist, as Christ did, on calling sin by its name, you'll have to be prepared for smiles. Sin is not an *in* word any more. Even if it's a very *in* thing.

The world has got very understanding about sin, very broad-minded and bland. What *you're* going to have to remember is that Christ left us a moral code. Things are right and things are wrong, and generally we know the one from the other. When we're doubtful, there is a reliable authority to tell us (you will forgive the word authority; it is not used any longer in polite conversation). The awkward thing is that you can feel in a minority when you insist that right is not wrong, nor wrong right. And you have to get used to this.

You'll understand your position better, though, if you reflect that for Christ's people, things have always been like this. Things like profiteering, dishonesty, marital infidelity, murder of the unborn, drunkenness – they are not new inventions like, say, satellite communication. They were there all around the first Christians. The first Christians had to reject them, unequivocally. And that is what they did. It made them different. It isolated them. They stood out, clean and strong, from the human degradation that surrounded them. That was the whole point. It still is. Christ's people were *meant* to be different.

Why not be a missionary?

Fame is – not – the spur

(June 1986)

That year my photograph appeared on the front page of *l'Osservatore Romano*, perhaps many thousands of ardent readers around the world looked upon my glory and wondered, but if they did they never told me. The papal delegate was about the only one in my area who ever saw the paper, and since hardly anyone else I knew had enough Italian to read about my accomplishments, I was effectively preserved from the pitfalls of pride and self-complacency. I don't know where *l'Osservatore* got the picture – there is no controlling one's fans in certain stages of enthusiasm – but I have to confess that the editors had a nice sense of history. The occasion of the photograph was an all-time *first*, and I am thankful that, seeing they were going to put me on permanent record, they at least did it then, when I was doing what I was doing.

What I was doing was accepting the offerings from a long line of professional people at the proper point in a big liturgical celebration. It was the first ever World Communications Day, and the journalists, printers, broadcasters, writers, commentators, distributors, producers, engineers – a pretty fair cross-section of the media people in the city, in fact – carried their typewriters, pens and pads, microphones, screwdrivers, car keys, ink pots, alarm clocks, anything that symbolised the job they did or the urgency that ruled their lives; and they laid them down upon a table in front of the altar, making an offering of them that we all hoped would be an acceptable accompaniment to the offering of the Mass itself.

We are fully convinced of it now, of course, but that was early days. When the word came from afar that we were expected to get this *Day* celebration off the ground because the Vatican Two *Decree on Communications* had prescribed it, we cast around for ways to make it significant. It was a *first* remember, and we did not have any precedents to guide us. I cannot recall that anyone realised at the time that the first concrete results of the Vatican Council were the *Constitution on the Liturgy* and the *Decree on the Instruments of Social Communications*; both published on the same day in 1963, so that was hardly the reason why we immediately mixed the communications people into the liturgy. No, I think it was just that we lived in the midst of a very religious-minded people, and the thought of celebrating *anything* without bringing it to church for a start would hardly have occurred to them or to us.

Still, I got a surprise at the response when we put the suggestion around that the media folk might like to bring along their tools of the trade and have them included in the offertory of the Mass. The idea was an instant success. And it was not just our *own* folk in the Catholic community that were interested; the thing became a quite notable ecumenical occasion. It was not possible to bring along the big rotary presses on which the dailies were printed, but we had fonts of type, printers' mallets, scissors and paste, tape recorders, broadcasters' scripts, and copies of the Sunday papers, the weekly bulletins and the monthly magazines, as well as the very latest news item – torn off the teleprinter of a wire service while the story was still running.

When we gathered afterwards in a hall nearby for a friendly drink and a speech or two to round off the event, everyone was enthusiastic that we should make this an annual thing. The media people we so frequently tangled with, it turned out, quite liked being treated like human beings worthy of esteem, and even if some of them manifested surprise that anyone should think their work worthy of being offered to God, the idea very evidently appealed to them, and probably brought a new dimension into their lives.

It was to be still four or five years before the great new pastoral instruction on communications was published, so we had yet to hear the press, radio, television and cinema described as *lifeless instruments,* but that Sunday in the cathedral and later in the school hall, I think we had the idea. Certainly, there were a lot of powerful new tools around, but the use that was going to be made of them depended on the people at the controls. People like these, with careers to develop in a very competitive world, with families to support, and bills to pay, with deadlines to meet and with urgencies pressuring them. Human beings, no stronger and no weaker than the rest of us ... but expected to deliver maybe a lot more than can be expected of us ... truth, inspiration, guidance, encouragement, timely information, entertainment, comfort in season, even admonition ... Maybe they elected themselves to these responsibilities, but even so, they must have some sort of natural right to pastoral support, and a friendly prayer from the consumers who devour them.

Why not be a missionary?

For this time only

(July/August 1986)

Whenever he gets the chance, the doctor tells me that I am not a racing car and that I therefore do not absolutely have to go from zero to one-hundred-and-fifty miles per hour in seven seconds, and would I therefore try to be my age and take my time. So now, instead of hurtling out of the bed in the mornings as though it were on fire (as I was taught by the best authorities to do in the earliest days of my training), I obediently accustom myself to roll to a sitting position on the edge without haste and then to check all systems before proceeding to dress. I find I like getting up this way a lot more than I used to doing it the old way, and the reason is that whereas previously I hardly ever thought about how well I was feeling and how good it was to be alive this bright morning, now I take time and thought to *enjoy* feeling great.

More than that, when I have satisfied myself that I have no ache or pain, or at least none that I can't live with fairly comfortably, the next thing I turn to is the state of the world, and here it is usually a different story. So many aches and pains, so many wars and enmities, so many disasters, such foolishness, such wickedness, so much pride and stubbornness, so much futile debate, such waste of energy, such stupid sterile hate, such soul-shrinking greed ...

I was already writing this, line by painful line, when the story broke about the nuclear problem in Ukraine, and then it was only a day or two before people began for the first time in history, probably, to look with baleful suspicion at their cabbage; and everyone became a meteorological authority overnight, with wise reflections on wind directions, precipitations, radiation levels and decontamination procedures. So I watched, listened to, and read media as they wrung the last drop of sensation, agony, anger, fear, righteous indignation, political advantage, ideological justification, and even religious significance, out of the story ...

Also, you should know, it just so happened that, for the first time in a rather generously chequered career, I was writing something, namely this gem of literature you are reading, on a computer, watching every mistake I made on the unfamiliar keyboard come up instantly on the screen and finding out with a lot of effort how to make electronic corrections. And I quickly discovered that this was much more fun than just beating an ordinary typewriter or pushing a pen ... apart from keeping me on even terms with every ten-year-old programmer I meet on the road!

You think I'm rambling, don't you? Well maybe, but that's the way my mind works between starting to get up and finishing my washing and dressing. I am giving you the authentic picture. Also God comes into it a lot, and other immediate things – and this morning as well there was the business of putting together what I was to say later to a man and woman who would be sharing Mass with me today on the sixtieth anniversary of their marriage.

What I will say to them is more or less the same thing I keep on saying to myself: how wonderful to be given our lives to live *now,* in this time, in the world as it is today! How wonderful not to have exhausted all the surprises, or made all the discoveries, or plumbed all the depths, or scaled all the heights, or learned all the knowledge, or seen the end of invention, or passed the last challenge! How wonderful to be a *witness* – because you are a Christian – to everything good and beautiful, in the world just as it is, today, and maybe tomorrow, and maybe even for a long while yet, and from here to the ends of the earth. How wonderful, most of all, to know you have great stories to tell, and that you have more, much *much* more, still to *give!*

Why not be a missionary?

... Over the hill

(June 1987)

There comes a time, maybe you will be lucky enough to reach it, when your friends (assuming you have any left) begin sending you droll birthday cards with messages like: 'Who cares if you're worn out and knackered! We'll gladly put up with you another while ...' If they are specially close – as the children of your closest friends tend to be – they are liable to make jocular references to your *degeneration*, telling you not to worry, it happens to everyone. As if they knew anything about it, bless them!

The irony is – well, there are several ironies about this aspect of life, so let's list some of them. One is that getting long in the tooth creeps up on you ... (ahem!); the calendar says one thing, but your internal barometer recognises no such *low:* you sit securely in your personal anticyclone, and you feel precisely, tranquilly, the same, today, tomorrow, five years later, quietly planning for the year 2000 like the rest of them, and far beyond.

The fact that your contemporaries disappear from the scene in increasing numbers doesn't really make the impact on you that might be expected; first of all, you seldom get round to thinking of them as dead, but even when you make the effort, you don't seem to make the obvious connections; you just accept with admirable resignation that, at their age, their departure was not too surprising. And of course you say a prayer for them!

If you look in a mirror, it is more likely to be because you want somebody sensible to talk to, or as a means of checking whether you are in a fit state to meet your public, than because you have any compulsion to study the ravages of time. In any case, the mirror's message is so gently graded and gradual that you seldom get shocks or revelations from it. Same old three and fourpence, you'd probably conclude, if you chanced to think about it. And it's always been reliably there when you looked ...

It gets to you, of course, but intellectually first, and on the whole, pleasantly. (Someone should put up a notice: Ageing is fun.) It gets to you chiefly when you look back, probably because it *can* be a little startling to realise how *far* back, all of a sudden, you can look! Startling – and very joyful. And there are two reasons for the joy, at least two ...

There is an old Jesuit prayer-method in which you look at the twists and turns your life has taken back along the way and try to see how God was operating in his own wise loving way at every point. (In the hilarious new language of spirituality, this is called studying your *personal graced history.* Jeepers!) It is a very joyful thing to observe God's love in your life, to see how it has headed you off and turned you round and hedged you about and repaired so much of the damage caused by your studies, and somehow kept you following one shining crazy star to this very day.

This very day, that's the second joyful thing you discover along with the startling realisation of your advancing years. You begin to take the days separately, and every one of them is a bonus and a new surprise. Worn out you may be and knackered, at least to external appearances, but the living gets daily more intense. There are so many things you want to do, so many demands on every precious minute. There is such a new urgency to build the *kingdom,* such brilliant fresh insights on how to do it, so many exciting new tools, so many techniques to learn, such compensations to be made for past lethargy ... Today, this wonderful, *graced,* unearned – and unearnable – today is possibly all the time you've got. It has twenty-four hours. Who has time to grow old!

Why not be a missionary?

A great gospel

(January/February 1988)

I hate to disappoint you right here on the threshold of the New Year, but if you were expecting me to join the chorus and give you a weighty (or even witty) discourse on the Third Millennium, all you are going to get is the correct spelling (two 'i's and two 'n's), and up to a minute ago I did not know even that for sure. No, I don't think I am going to be ready to pronounce on the year 2000 at least until I have come to terms with 1987 and got myself properly launched on 1988.

Something unexpected and bothersome turned up during 1987. There were too many mornings, I found, when I didn't like the gospel of the day; or when some of the sentiments expressed in it came across to me as somehow a little unfortunate! Early on many a morning I felt the rasp of the hard sayings of Jesus, and almost reacted with a hurt: *How could you?* There had to be something wrong with me. Had I been paying too much attention to the *world* and been absorbing its values? Or had I been listening too uncritically to alluring voices preaching only the parts of the gospel that made hardly any demands? And the disturbing thought occurred to me: What kind of gospel have I myself been preaching; can I have been toning it down to suit the popular expectation?

The *offending* gospel had to have been St Luke's; we were reading from that most weekdays in '87. But how could Luke possibly rasp? ... the parables of mercy, the whole nativity story, Christ eating and drinking with outcasts, making much of small children, Christ weeping over Jerusalem, visiting Mary and Martha, telling us that we must look for the kingdom of God in our own midst ... Certainly none of that was any trouble. No, but I had recollections of short bitty little gospel readings which ended with rebukes or even threats and sent you into the day with a flea in your ear ... 'fear him who has power to cast you soul and body into hell', 'whoever is ashamed of me and of my words, of him will the Son of Man be ashamed when he comes in his glory', 'he who is not with me is against me', 'unless you repent, you will all perish like those people', 'none of these invited shall taste of my banquet', 'tax collectors passing you by into heaven and you yourselves thrust out' ...

Yes, that was it. All these hard sayings were certainly there, and more besides, and there was no point at all in pretending I liked them. But it was the first time I had ever felt even a little resentful about them. Perhaps what was wrong was that the extracts for some of the days were really too bitty, and you got them out of context in the wan morning when what you needed was hope and encouragement …

The cure, you'd have thought, was to read the whole gospel slowly and prayerfully and reflectively, and get everything in context. I do not do it that way. I sat down with the gospel according to Luke and read it at one sitting, very fast, really skimming, in fact, in several places, letting myself get the *feeling* of Jesus Christ, Son of God and Son of Man. It was quite wonderful, story piled on story, quick shifts of scene and situation, and Christ there at every point, talking with great energy and sureness, laying out with no ambivalence at all the programme of life you and I must follow if we wish to *taste at his banquet* at the end. It was all so coherent and direct, such a straightforward laying of all the cards on the table, that it made nonsense of the half-conscious objections I had been nursing. This, all this together, was Christianity, and it was possible, and it was great.

If you really want to warm yourself here in the wan wonderful dawn of the New Year, and get a clearer idea of an overall programme that will make it a great year, why don't you just do what I did! Take St Luke's gospel and read it fast, at one sitting if you can. Pieces of it will stay with you: 'Take heed to yourselves lest your hearts be weighed down with dissipation and drunkenness and the cares of this life …', 'Fear not, little flock … make for yourselves purses that do not grow old, with a treasure in heaven that does not fail, where no thief approaches and no moth destroys; for where your treasure is, there is your heart also'. 'If anyone will come after me, let him deny himself, and take up his cross, every day, and follow me', 'blessed is that servant whom the master when he comes finds awake'. For you and for me, 1988 can be the year of the gospel – the whole gospel. We'll meet the third millennium when we come to it.

Why not be a missionary?

What's in a face?

(June 1988)

I'm walking slowly down a very long corridor, so long that at the rate I'm travelling, it is going to take me most of an hour to reach the far end. There is no hurry, though. When I reach the far end, I am just going to turn round and spend another hour coming back. I don't often have a chance to visit a place like this, but when I do, I like to be alone so that I can do it at my own pace, and think whatever thoughts come to me till I've thought them through.

I am in the main sculpture gallery of an enormous museum, and right down the length of that long corridor, on both sides, and here and there even in the middle, are lined hundreds and hundreds of marble heads. Some of them have whole bodies attached, others just a neck or chest. What is fascinating to me is that all of them were sculpted two thousand years ago, give or take a couple of centuries, and that pretty nearly all were sculpted from life, that is, they are portraits of real persons. They were born and lived and died. Just a few were public people, emperors and the like, about whom I know a little from books. Whatever I can piece together about the others, the great silent unknown majority, I must read from their faces. So I move slowly along, looking closely, attentively, into these faces one by one.

I discover something: you get a clearer idea about people when you view them from different angles. Again and again, after I've made up my mind about the type of person I am looking at, I change position and get the face in profile, and there instantly I see an extra little something: maybe a cluster of laugh lines near the eyes, or a pucker of what may be bad temper on a brow, a sardonic twist to the lips, a little more generosity, a suggestion of cruelty, sensitivity, self-satisfaction, pettishness, endurance, dependability, honesty, discontent, or simple happiness.

'What about you ... what have you to say for yourself?' I ask a calm fearless face. I hear the man (or anyway my own judgment of him) replying: 'One thing I will claim before the world: I tell the truth. Strictly. No fibs, no white lies, no prevarications, mental reservations, distortions, exaggerations, understatements.

The truth. I tell it *as it is*. To you. To myself. About myself. About you. About every one and about everything …' I take a longer look and I say: 'Yes, I can believe that about you.' I move on, warmed and astonished.

'And you?', I ask a compassionate noble face farther down the row. 'I practise justice,' the face says silently back to me. 'I claim no more than that, but I practise it strictly. What's yours is yours, not mine. Your toothpaste, your loose change, your books, records, tapes, your leather coat, tools, machines, shopping bags full and empty, your right of way, your right to have an opinion, your right to walk the roads, day or night, unmolested. Your right to have your secrets, your good name, your particular faith …'

And he goes on (or I go on – I'm not sure which!): 'I'll grant you the anachronism, but why does the rest astonish you – I may have been an early Christian, and the practice of strict justice was a demand of my faith, as it is of yours, brother!'

It gets to me, what he is suggesting. Very many of these people walked the earth when the faith was young. Any one of them can easily have been a link in the chain that passed the faith on to me. And look in the other direction! A thousand, or two thousand, or ten thousand years from now, people yet unborn may chance upon an image of me (maybe a primitive colour photograph that represents the state of the art in the 1980s), and may look at me attentively and form an estimate regarding what manner of person I was – and never once suspect that the faith they profess came down the line directly from me to them. And it will not matter at all that they do not know. But the truth and the justice and the love and goodness of the lives they lead will matter a great deal.

Why not be a missionary?

A club to join

(July/August 1988)

There is an incredible passage in the Acts of the Apostles where the rulers of the people are having a meeting, trying to decide how to deal with a group of pesky followers of the late Jesus who are going around telling people that he is back in circulation, alive and well. To compound the nuisance, it has now been found that a couple of them have worked some kind of cure on a crippled man right at the temple gate, where it was sure to get the maximum publicity, and are now claiming that they've done it simply by *faith in his name,* that is, in the name of the said Jesus deceased. Then comes the incredible bit:

'They conferred with one another, saying, "What shall we do with these men? For that a notable sign has been performed through them is manifest to everyone, and we cannot deny it. But in order that it may spread no further among the people, let us warn them to speak no more to anyone in this name ...".' (Acts 4:16, 17)

So they threatened and warned, apparently blind to the implications of their own argument. The apostles, however, were having none of it. It is a choice between what God says and what you are saying, they argued; what do you *expect* us to do? And back they went merrily to their preaching, and ... 'many of those who heard the word believed ... and the number came to about five thousand'.

A funny kind of cat-and-mouse game now developed. Into jail, out of jail, you were never quite sure where you were going to find the apostles. Slap them in irons tonight, and there they are preaching about Jesus in the temple in the morning. How did they get out? An angel of the Lord 'opened the doors and brought them out' no less! Arrest them again, and they cheerfully seize the occasion to turn their trial into a preaching session ... 'the God of our fathers raised Jesus whom you killed ... to give repentance and forgiveness of sins ... and *we are witnesses to these things, and so is the Holy Spirit whom God has given* ...' No ranting or raving; just a calm declaration from which they are not going to back down.

The rulers' reaction was somewhat less calm and measured

... 'they were enraged and wanted to kill them'! ... Enter Gamaliel, the wise lawyer-Pharisee respected by all the people: 'Take care what you do with these men,' he says, 'let them alone; for if this plan or this undertaking is of God, you will not be able to overthrow them, and you'll be in opposition to God. If it's merely something dreamed up by men, you need not worry about it; it will fail of itself.' They listened to Gamaliel, but they beat the apostles anyway before letting them go, maybe just out of spite, maybe to keep them careful. No use! They walked out *rejoicing,* and next thing you knew, they were back in the temple, fearlessly *teaching and preaching Jesus as the Christ.*

And it is into this tradition that you are invited, urged, dared, to put yourself and everything you've got: youth, middle age, declining years, energies, ideals, dreams, life. Gamaliel, you should note, saw a long way beyond his nose. His instinct was right when he judged that *this plan or undertaking* could not be suppressed or overthrown. He may not have known by what name to call it, but he was certain the gospel, if it was really God's *good news,* was not going to go away – ever. Could he possibly have guessed too, as he estimated the calibre and conviction of the cheerful group in the dock, that their breed would endure a thousand years, and longer, much longer?

It has anyway. A club you can join.

Why not be a missionary?

Buzz words

(June 1989)

Diaries come in many shapes and sizes. Each Christmas I acquire a fair variety of makes and models as gifts from kind friends. Each January I spend a little time unloading these on other people. In the end I go out and buy one for myself. I can do without the signs of the zodiac, the tables of weights and measures, the metric conversion tables, the car registration codes, and the expensive padded leather covers. What I must have is a size and weight that will fit comfortably in my baggage when I travel, and an arrangement of the space which gives me one whole week on two facing pages.

There are two principal ways to keep a diary. One way is to write down each night in greater or less detail what you have been doing in the day just ending. This way looks to the past. The other method (which looks to the future) is to write reminders to yourself in the appropriate spaces so that you'll know where you are supposed to be and have some notion what you're supposed to be doing tomorrow and next Wednesday week and on the nineteenth and twenty-sixth of August coming.

Since it has always seemed to me that the future is where the action is, my diaries have tended to follow the second method, but sometimes there is a note tagged on to a particular entry to confirm that the appointment was in fact kept, or the bill paid, or the plane caught, or the anniversary remembered. Mostly, however, the note tagged on is just a key word which will recall something that caught the imagination, or was specially moving or exciting or memorable. (It is very frustrating indeed when the entry is so cryptic, or the scribble so illegible, that I am unable to figure out what I was saying to myself in 1972 or 1969 ... and who can tell what treasures of recollection have been lost through this breakdown in communication?)

The single word *Perahera* gives instant recall to a marvellous mountain town with a lake in the middle where the family elephant stood chewing the cud – or whatever elephants chew – tethered in little gardens beside people's houses along the streets; and people drove around in tidy little cars with smartly trotting buffaloes between the shafts; it recalls the Temple of the Tooth, where little children came with radiant faces to offer flower petals to the Buddha on their upturned palms; the great procession in the night of the caparisoned elephants, three by three, with hundreds of costumed dancers in between, and drums, music, incense, fireworks.

The word *Reef!* (with an exclamation mark) refers to a plane journey in high summer northward from Sydney to Papua New Guinea. The Great Barrier Reef, long heard about and now much anticipated, was directly underneath for miles – and this *had* to be the one freak day when it was totally hidden by thick cloud. A little way along: a clear, clear, sunny sky, and visibility so marvellous that you could see down to the bottom of the sea ...

There are many other words: *Tandem,* I remember, refers to the two bicycles-for-two seen in a mission store in Kenya. There were no wheels; people pedalled to drive a little mill for grinding maize. The mill was on the front handlebars. *Biechy* refers to the big red cathedral glimpsed one very early morning down a long street in Brazzaville in the Congo. This had to be *Biechy's* cathedral, and I got excited seeing it. *Biechy* was the legend to end all legends in the place where I first went missioneering, a bearded Frenchman out of the distant past who to my people was and would always be the greatest. They could have been right, judging by what he had left behind when he was transferred south to be a bishop in Brazzaville.

It comes to me that people who keep diaries as I do can quickly become very great bores. The entries are cryptic, but the stories they suggest are the sort that can go on for ever, gathering fuel with every new association they cast up.

The thing you've got to realise, of course, is that between the entries there are lots and lots of blank spaces, sometimes whole blocks of blank pages. The blank pages, in general, represent the times when you weren't going anywhere, or seeing anything out of the ordinary, or meeting anyone you felt you should make notes about, or doing anything at all spectacular. The blanks are probably the sections that God reads with special attention, maybe even with most approval. Why? Because the routine days when you were just doing your ordinary job as a matter of course and living as well as you could by the principles and ideals you elected to live by – without giving it any special thought or making a very big deal out of it – the key word for these in God's book might easily be *fidelity*. That could be worth a lot of elephants!

Why not be a missionary?

Who, me?

(November 1989)

I had a cousin once who was also a specially close friend, and she was married to a marvellous man whom she loved very dearly despite the fact that he sometimes mistakenly believed that he knew what was best for them both. And there was one memorable evening when he insisted that he could get her home faster by driving through the centre of a town which was having a *fleadh ceoil*. She liked to relate how, hours later, as she sat under the gaze of helpless police in the middle of a hopelessly jammed main street, with big friendly men drinking pints off the roof of the car, even her feet were blushing.

There came a time when I understood exactly what she meant. There was an urgent message to be delivered by hand to someone very important, and the only way it could be got through the crush was to send the messenger in an official car with a police escort. I was elected messenger, for no good reason other than the fact that I was, like Mount Everest, *there,* and as such, in a convenient position to be ordered around. The available car was a mile long. As passenger, I sat in a rear section designed to give maximum exposure and sufficiently separated from the uniformed driver to indicate that I was not like the rest of men. A thing I will never understand is why, when I have a nightmare, it never features sirens and flashing lights and the contemptuous eyes of resentful multitudes hating me, for an imposter, through plate glass. Hanging by the fingernails three quarter ways up an unscalable cliff may relate to some buried fear in my subconscious, but it can in no way compare with the indescribable horror of that crosstown trip.

Reflecting on it all these years later I say to the Lord: 'The things I do for you ...!' and a sort of Don Camillo dialogue ensues: 'Why do you say it was for me you went through this?' 'Well, I got caught in the situation because of what I am' ... 'But, you know, you could have sat up front with the driver' ... 'Oh thanks, *now* I could because I'm older and wiser and firmer about doing things my way; it was different then, you may remember.' 'How? ... how was it different?' 'I had this thing about doing not only *what* I was told, but *how* I was told. It seemed more perfect to do it *their* way.' 'I see ... but now it's more perfect to follow your own selfish inclinations in all things?' 'I didn't say selfish, nor in all things; these seem to me unfair generalisations ... oh look, let's drop this.'

'This piece really set out, as you know, Lord, to be a simple meditation on St Matthew. Now there's someone who got caught, wouldn't you say, in a lot of things he hardly expected, because of what he was. Same as I did! (But what he was, he was by his own choice, was he not?) Oh, come off it, Lord; haven't you ever looked at Caravaggio's picture, *The call of St. Matthew?* (Indeed I have, the original painting, in fact. But the date on that is about 1599, don't forget. And how does Caravaggio get to be an authority on a happening nearly sixteen hundred years back?) Easy, by reading the scriptures and using the imagination you Lord endowed him with.'

I find this recreation of the event convincing. There *you* are quite definitely saying, "Follow me", and there is Matthew Levi, startled out of his wits, quite evidently saying: "Who – *me?*" It must have been like that. And then, up he gets and follows you, and, sound man that he is, he celebrates his extraordinary decision by throwing a big party for you, and he's not ashamed to invite his disreputable friends either – and you, praise be, were not ashamed to be seen sitting down with them. You know, I think this is my favourite *vocation* story. Reminds me of some Legionaries of Mary coming to my parish long ago to recruit new members, and they surprised the parish priest by heading for the pub, where they recruited one or two of the local *hard men* and these turned out, to their own considerable surprise, to be gifted and powerful spreaders of faith and good works ...

But I digress. And of course, yes, Matthew's decision was Matthew's own decision. Nobody forced him to leave his job at the tax office. But you called him, Lord, in that way that was particular to him, and to him unmistakable. I don't suppose you'd deny that you helped him to give the right response? He didn't have to know at that stage that he'd have to write a gospel to keep the story straight, or that he'd lose his life bearing witness to it. I didn't have to know that I'd have to blush down to the feet at some of the situations I'd find myself in because of how I responded to the call that was special to *me* ... or that there would be some memorable parties along the way in celebration of so much that really didn't need then to be foreseen.

Why not be a missionary?

What can I bring?

(December 1989)

I'm looking back on the year, asking myself what, out of the mixum-gatherum of doings and goings and impressions, plannings and longings and experiences of those twelve months, I might bring as an offering to the crib.

It was a visit from a rather well-off woman I know that set me off on this: she came in a state of high excitement, and on the table between us she laid down a white box she was carrying, and she said, watching me closely for my triumphantly anticipated reaction: 'Just you look what I've got here!' So I looked.

Inside the box, resting snugly in a precisely sculpted nest of foam-rubber, was a milky-coloured round vase or flask with a long neck. It was not something that I would particularly want to live with. It was not sparkling lead-crystal. It was, in fact, dull, opaque and discoloured. But then she explained that the object was an exact replica of one of the pieces of ancient Roman glassware which are preserved, of all places, in the Vatican Library. It was a collector's piece. She had been searching frantically for a suitable present for some friend of hers, and to her great delight had stumbled upon, as she put it, 'the perfect gift for someone who has everything'.

The mind's eye, I find, has its own playback system, and a phrase like that can set off the mechanism. I began to get pictures of swarthy men on camels, *wise men from the east,* carefully holding golden boxes on their saddle pommels. Gold, frankincense and myrrh: gifts for a king, for a God, for someone who was human and who therefore was to die. Gifts for someone who had everything ... and nothing. Gifts for a baby, warm, loved and secure, in a manger, in a stable.

What do I bring him out of all my year? This year I've seen gold, so much gold that it did not seem precious any more, in a famous museum that had nothing else to show. This year I saw where the spices grow and the gums and resins for the incense; where the salt is mined from the mountains and evaporated from the sea. I've seen a droop-winged Concorde on a runway, grown flowers, gone on pilgrimages, swum in warm seas, read books, listened to lectures, prayed, condoled, laughed, preached, mourned, been robbed, been deeply moved by goodness and badness, given, received, met with the great and the little, sweated immoderately in sweltering heat, been rained upon, been resented, been cold, been spoiled with kindness and taken for granted and left out of things and dragged into things. This year I've worked, and it's been sometimes joy, sometimes drudgery. I've been happy with friends. I've been happy being a priest. I've been happy being a missionary, I've been happy just being! What do I bring of all this?

There was that hot day in July, speeding in a beat-up *Malaga* along the base of Montserrat, a formidable mountain in Catalonia whose cruel peaks rake the sky like the teeth of a comb. Squinting up the dizzy rockface to the point infinitely above, where the old Abbey was just discernible against the sameness of the surrounding stone masses, I remembered that monks had been living their lives out, up there, for nearly a thousand years. 'What keeps them there?' I asked myself, knowing the answer in a general way. 'I know they've got vows to keep, but vows by themselves couldn't hold them,' I remarked to the other occupants of the car. I turned to the Mexican girl, the teacher in a university who for all her twenties and now into her thirties, gives all her free time to prayer and to serving the old and the poor. 'You have no vows, Letizia, so what holds you to this kind of life?' I asked her. The answer came without hesitation, *'la mia libertà,'* ... my own free choice ... my own willing gift ... it's because I want to ... (how do you translate it so as to say what she intended?) ...

Maybe it just about sums it up, for the monks on Montserrat, and for all the dedicated people who crossed my path this year, even for me away down there at the end of the parade. For what it's worth, our willing gift it is what *we* can bring on our saddle pommels.

Why not be a missionary?

The real man

(March 1990)

Moiling around in my head was a welter (if a welter can indeed moil) of semi-formulated notions about St Patrick that I was planning to sort out and write down in view of his approaching feast; but when I sat down to write, I got derailed straight away by the inscription on a black-bordered card that chanced to be looking up at me from beside the keyboard:

'May he support us all the day long (the card said), till the shades lengthen and the evening comes and the busy world is hushed and the fever of life is over and our work is done, then in his mercy may he give us a safe lodging and a holy rest and peace at the last.' (Cardinal Newman)

So *Amen* to all that, for a start. The other side of the card has the photograph of an old friend and colleague, with the date when life began for him and the date – sadly recent – when it ended. He knew all about *the fever of life*, of that I have been a witness, and I have seen him more than once burning with another kind of fever, the routine bout of malaria that hits some of us because of how and where we are, and halts and slows us in our gallop till we've sweated it out.

He'd get up afterwards and go on, a trifle unsteadily at first, a little wan and fine drawn; sure however that he would survive as often before, regain strength, return to normal operating mode. That's the way it was through all the years of his purposeful, undramatic, unrelentingly productive missionary life. When he died – wouldn't you know it! – it was something else that got him, and it was sudden. He'll be missed, by me, by many. It will be easy to envy him the life he lived, and that he lived it, really *lived* it, till he died, probably never even noticing that the shades were lengthening and the evening coming and the busy world hushing, *et cetera*. 'What a way to go ...'

The thought of it helps answer a question for me. A priest I met before Christmas – a Jesuit he was, from somewhere in deepest Sicily – asked me for a picture of St Patrick. When I got back to my sources, I searched around for one to send him. But which shall it be of those available? This *foreigner* is, you might say, *coming in cold*, in no way *conditioned* by childhood memories of green robes, Celtic scrolls, snakes, wolfhounds, round towers, or large shamrock-shaped badges saying: *Kiss me I'm Irish*.

The picture I send should make Patrick real for him, introduce him to the great man that really was, ploughing his deep lasting furrow far from home, sweat on his face, pain sometimes in his eyes, stubborn, gentle, homesick, contemplative, hurt and healed, betrayed and unembittered, oh, and with something enduring about him making it certain he'd still be there at sundown, or until the job was done. The picture should show someone with a vision that will never let him give up.

The nearest thing I've got shows a faded sort of bishop with sweat-bleared eyes and a somehow de-emphasised mitre. He is in a very golden, very ripe cornfield, and his big hands are clamped on his staff as a reaper might have clamped them, knuckle-wristed and gaunt, on the shaft of his scythe, stopping a moment to rest. I know a bishop with a faded look like that in the glare of a desert, vulnerable, indestructible; he could have posed for this. I well remember raw-boned hands like those coaxing life into dead engines for me long ago in a sub-Sahara mission. I remember how a young missionary had to struggle to get his leg across a motor-cycle, and how he used hold himself like this Patrick in the picture, careful of his back; and how well he got over his *bit of rheumatism* so many years later – with artificial hip-joints …

Sorry, this picture brings back a lot of things. Spend a lifetime with people who have, broadly, been living Patrick's sort of life, for Patrick's sort of reasons, and doubtless under his urging and tutelage: it shouldn't be too surprising that some things about him seem terribly familiar. My friend from Sicily won't get all this: he may think the picture is about the past, whereas it is more about the present, and a lot more about the future.

Why not be a missionary?

Love in the morning

(May 1990)

There was a while when I had to live with a PC, or personal computer, which was connected into a kind of central system shared by several other people. This meant that I was able to work into and out of a very big *memory*, which was an advantage, but it also meant that I couldn't entirely control my own destiny and had to put up with various minor irritants. For instance, when I switched on my desk unit of a morning, right away I was liable to get a chatty message on the screen, like: *Good morning Father Glynn. I am pleased to be working with you. You are station Five. It's Monday ... aaarrrrgh! ... but try to have a nice day anyway.* There was a different message for Saturdays, which included, I think, *Yippee!*

Well, you don't need a machine to dictate what feelings and reactions are appropriate for you at given times, but neither do you want to hurt a programmer who likes introducing a little good cheer into the working day; so I tried to absorb the jolly remarks with simplicity and a good grace, till the system eventually went haywire and we regressed to working on floppy discs, each of us secure in his individual corner. Before the nuisance abated, though, it did something unexpected for me. It made Monday friendly, and the successive days each a separate marvel. Because, must it not, I reflected, be some kind of blasphemy (or, at any rate, boorish bad manners, which may be nearly as bad and feels even worse!), to make complaining noises in the morning – any morning?

It happened that, where I was living, Vatican Radio used to come in strong on medium wave around midnight with a long programme of very listenable music – *With you in the night* – which was agreeable to go to sleep to. At intervals the music was gently faded to ease in a deeply resonant male voice doing a short reading, usually from Psalm 92:

It is good to give thanks to the Lord
To make music to your name, O Most High,
To proclaim your love in the morning
And your truth in the watches of the night ...

As a prayer for night-owls, this is hard to beat, especially when it comes with music, and it rather spontaneously became my dreamy going-to-sleep sign-off as the mists closed in. But the notion of proclaiming *love in the morning* appealed even more, and I began to find I was switching on the working day, Monday or Saturday as might be, on a note of quite genuine exultancy. Psalm 92 had the right words for that, too:

Your deeds, O Lord, have made me glad;
For the work of your hands I shout with joy!

There is so much (I would tell myself), so very much, to shout about – and with joy: God's *deeds* in my own life, and what I have actually seen of *the work of his hands* in other peoples. And if sometimes I wake up wondering where am I today (as happens when you wander the earth a lot), I wake up – always and everywhere the same – to the familiar nearness of the God who gives me life, and to the certainty that I matter to him. Wherever I am, we are together – and I hope that maybe it will show as the hours pass. A few glad shouts repeated down the day will help to keep the mood alive, and the scowl off the face, and the whine out of the voice ... his love is not just for the morning.

Am I talking maybe about prayer? Let's be on the safe side and say only that it's what passes for prayer in my life. Yours may be deeper, richer and more solemn, to be sure, and that's fine with me; but if it's heavy-hearted – I say this without offence – I'm glad it's not mine. A book I was reading lately, by a good man from America whose work I admire, was called *Enjoy the Lord*. It said that when we get to heaven and see God face to face, from there on our normal state is going to be ecstasy. Our normal state! When you think about it, you'll realise that of course this has to be true; but have you ever heard anybody say it before? I haven't. So then ... if you, or I, or all of us, feel pretty good in his company even now, and even here, wherever on land or sea or in the air we find ourselves, is that really so very weird or strange?

Why not be a missionary?

A Christmas *Yes*

(*December 1990*)

I once got a – richly deserved – slap on the wrist from a nun, and it happened in this way. The meaning of one of the bidding prayers she had composed to be read out by the novices at Mass had, frankly, escaped me, and I was curious to know whether it had made sense to anybody else, so I asked the sacristy Sister afterwards how she had understood it. She did not answer my question directly. She simply said: 'Well, you know, Sister So-and-So is a theologian ...' as if that explained everything. However, the word got back to Sister So-and-So that I had enquired, and some time later there was delivered to me a note. It said simply: '2 Cor. 1:20'. When I looked this up, I was suitably chastened to find that Paul in his Second Letter to the Corinthians used the same formula of words read out by the novice during the Prayers of the Faithful.

So game, set and match to Sister So-and-So, and I shall always bless her for having caused me to look a bit more closely at this passage of scripture ... because it has helped me to see a lot more clearly what I am looking at when I visit the crib at Christmas.

The passage had to do with being a person of your word, with saying *yes* when you mean *yes* and *no* when you mean *no*. Paul is quite prickly about his reputation in this regard. Nobody's going to be allowed to call him a *yes/no* man. His *yes* means *yes* and his *no* means *no* and – as they say where I come from – 'there's no two ways about that'.

What's more, 'the Son of God,' says Paul, 'Jesus Christ, whom we preached among you' – there's no yes-and-no nonsense about him! And then Paul says a strange and lovely thing. He says: 'In him it is always yes. For all the promises of God find their yes in him.'

In him it is always *yes*. He doesn't throw cold water on people's enthusiasms. He doesn't put people down. He doesn't expect instant perfection. He doesn't write us off once and for all when we have come our hundred-and-twenty-fifth cropper after one hundred and twenty-four times resolving-promising-swearing-our-bible-oath that *no, never again* ... He doesn't break the bruised reed or quench the smoking flax. He comes to save, not to condemn. He does not *knock,* he affirms. He says, *yes,* because: can I say it again? ... in him it is always *yes* ... for all the promises of God find their *yes* in him.

Somewhere I've read that in Roman churches at Mass in early Christian times, the people's *Amen* to the 'through him, with him, in him' was like a thunderclap. That's the time to shout. (I wish people would!) That is saying *yes* – today's *yes* – *yes* for our time – our *yes* – to the glory Christ is giving to the Father.

But I want to be, need to be, silent at the crib. I want just to light a candle there. It's the only thing I can think of to do. The crib leaves me wordless. What can I possibly say in response to the reality it spells out for me, to the proposition that Christ was able to say *yes* to? For I know I am getting it right; it is idiot-proof. In Christ's mind I was worth becoming incarnate for, worth living for, worth dying for, worth rising from the dead for, worth coming again for at the end which is the beginning, worth keeping by his side for ever thereafter ... I like to light my candle before that *yes,* let it burn for me there in the white silence where only the Holy Spirit speaks – in words beyond all utterance.

Christ who is the *yes* to all God's promises can find me there in the silence. He can affirm me, reach me with his nod as he reached each of the twelve that morning he put his team together, signalling in a way special to me out of all the world. He can take my old promises, and dust them off, and *yes,* say *yes* to them again. *Yes* meaning, *yes,* follow me! – a while longer! – in your own tinpot way!

Why not be a missionary?

No ifs and buts

(March 1991)

It seems that all my life I've been hearing people lament about that boy in the gospel who *went away sad*. The rich young man, to hear them tell it, was any mother's dream; didn't drink, didn't smoke, didn't gamble or philander, gave no trouble at home, behaved like a gentleman in company, kept a clean tongue. So this prodigy came to Christ one day seeking a magic formula for perfection, and Christ, who doesn't ever underestimate people, at once gave him one that seemed very well designed for a lad of his sterling qualities ...

And the plain unvarnished fact of the matter is that he said, *no thank you*, without a whole lot of hesitation and smartly took himself off. Oh yes, but of course he was *sad* going away.

So now maybe you want to join the chorus of the centuries and lament over him? Poor little rich boy, he was trapped by property, *he had great possessions*. Was it not a little hard to expect him to give it all up and follow Christ! But – ah me! – think what a wonderful apostle he might have made ...

Baloney! He said, *No!* He found it in his business-like little heart to opt for the dollars, when he had a direct and explicit invitation to go along with Christ. We can think of him as kindly as we like, but we're well rid of him. He is not, and never was, in the same class as the apostles. Peter, Andrew, James or John, did not have great possessions, to be sure, but boats and nets were their living. They left the boats bobbing there on the water, and the nets drying nearby. They walked away with Christ ...

They must have grinned later on at Christ's response when other aspiring apostles grandly offered in public to follow him *anywhere and forever*. 'You've got to know I do not have any fixed abode,' he said. 'Foxes have. Birds have. I do not have ...' What was he saying, really? Forget about total security; you take your chances when you take the road with me. If you're to be free to do what we have to do, you can't stay anchored to possessions, to things, to places ...

You can't stay anchored to people, either, even to your own flesh and blood. Christ soon made that clear. 'Let the dead bury their dead,' he said, surprisingly, to a lad who offered to come along but just asked for time to bury his father, 'your business is to spread the news of the kingdom.' As though to say: the demand is immediate and does not brook delay. It leaves little space for mooning in the past. Christ was really putting it on the line for the applicant. He had to understand the kind of commitment that was expected of him. James and John must have exchanged a glance. They knew the feeling. They had left their father Zebedee with the hired staff in the family boat when they took off.

Christ mentioned the plough to another would-be apostle – this one must have been a country fellow. He just wanted to go and explain things to his family. Once you've put your hand to the plough, he was told, you don't stand there looking back. You shake up the oxen – or rev the tractor – and go to work making furrows.

Does it all sound tough and ruthless? Not when you're cold serious about following Christ and preaching the *good news* that heals and saves. To do that, clearly you've got to be free, as he had to be free. Clearly too, cutting the various ties can hurt and cost, with homesickness a life companion, and the missing of loved ones like an ache that never lets up.

You hear a little of this in the tone of Christ's voice when they tell him that his mother and brethren stand without, asking for him. 'Who is my mother and who are my brethren?', he asks wryly. And he murmurs as he looks at the faces of all those surrounding him: 'These folk are, now.'

Why not be a missionary?

More than the music

(November 1991)

Accept the word of a traveller with no sense of direction who has been known in his time to go north when he meant south. When you need information about trains you must catch, modest lodgings, or the cheapest and best basic eating, anywhere in Europe, target yourself on one – any one – of the knapsack-carrying youngsters who abound in every railway station, and ask your humble question. He (or she) will, if necessary, quickly assemble the whole cohort of that knowing fraternity; will produce from some obscure depth in the baggage a bulky three-year-old copy of an indispensable something called, *Let's Go*, and having searched in it a moment will consult his peers for experienced comment on the findings before he advises you.

It is then that the wise listen carefully. The kid with the Eurorail ticket and the worse-for-wear designer stubble has knowledge beyond his years, whether it be about getting there, or about surviving once you've arrived. Trust him, or *(mutatis mutandis)* trust her. There is a chivalry thing among this lot, a kind of shoestring freemasonry of the highway, and they have travellers' tales to tell, generally in monosyllables, that will do a lot for your education.

I sat with two of them on a very wet Sunday morning in the great cathedral they had led me to in a town on the railway between Munich and Vienna. Entering, I had tried the man at the door for any response to the name Fergal, otherwise Virgil, otherwise Virgilius, and had begun to wonder was this really Salzburg when none of the versions seemed to strike any chord. But then he brightened. I think you mean Saint Verghil, he said, (making it a hard 'g' – as in Gill & Macmillan): yes, his body is in the crypt, his statue is out in front. And so it was, with Peter and Paul, and someone named Rupert. Wearing a mitre he was, at that, my wandering scholar-Irishman from twelve hundred years back who built the original cathedral on this spot.

The acoustics in today's cathedral are about perfect. We were there two hours early to make sure we got places for the ten o'clock Mass, because it was to be a Mozart Mass with a wonderful English orchestra and choir providing the music. Sitting on a cold stone step, we were getting a Schubert Mass as we waited, a bonus we had not anticipated, any more than we had anticipated the thirty-minute homily in German to which we were now giving at least external attention. It was getting home to us that this was a regular Sunday Mass and that probably nobody in the strikingly attentive congregation was there just for the music.

The homily, like all good things, came to an end; some of the people moved; we got decent seats in the nave and eventually we got our Mozart Mass. It was *performed* as the composer must have intended, in the context of an actual Eucharistic celebration, beautiful beyond words in the setting of that wonderful church. For good measure, we got another homily in German, this one by a mitred bishop, no less, but he had compassion on our weakness and took only fifteen minutes.

It was during this homily that my wandering eye fastened on an inscription above the pulpit, and somehow everything came together. The words were: *Semen est verbum Dei* ... The seed is the word of God. Below were bronze panels: Jesus with the doctors in the temple, with Nicodemus who came by night, with the woman taken in adultery; the sower going out to sow, the apostles going out with the gospel ... and flanking all these the pre-gospel prophet-preachers, Isaiah and Ezekiel.

This bishop now preaching was casting the seed of God's word. His predecessor, my scholar-builder-missionary fellow countryman, resting below in the crypt since 784, travelled a long way to do the same, in his time. The musicians from England were singing it to the world with all their hearts, trumpeting it from the galleries, moving the hearts of a multitude, making the ground receptive. Tied in with all this in the emotion of the moment were the knapsack-laden throngs of wandering youngsters in all the stations, their strange streetwise innocence, their outreaching goodwill towards all the world, their kindness, their caring. How immeasurable might be the harvest, I was thinking, if some angel inspired them to go out sowing the seed that is the word of God!

Why not be a missionary?

With open arms

(December 1991)

There was a fire burning on the shore and the chilled fishermen, homing wearily out of the long disappointing night, saw through the dawn mists the outline of a figure standing by it. There was a fish roasting and there was bread, and then suddenly there were full nets and a joyous recognition and a welcome invitation to breakfast. But this is an Easter rather than a Christmas story, of course, and it was the Risen Christ who was doing the honours, not the soon-to-be born Christ in the womb. But mark you, it was the *same* Christ.

He would learn strong lessons from his mother, in the human way of his upbringing, about the sacredness of concern for guests, and there would come an occasion when she would insist upon this beyond the bounds of reason or possibility and – with her heart in her mouth, perhaps – call for a miracle: his first.

She would always feel for anyone without shelter, for anyone who could not count on a next meal, and indeed, for anyone without the means to offer hospitality, wine or bread or roof, to callers at the door. She would never forget this night or this arrival. Neither would Joseph ...

Do you know what it's like to have nowhere to go? I have an unpleasant memory of arriving battered and bedraggled once in Lisbon after a rough journey. The plane was cancelled and the relief aircraft then delayed by a breakdown and a long wait for a spare part. Much later, in the wan small hours, in a hotel just off the generous street they call the Liberdade, they told me with little evidence of regret that they had given away the room I'd booked and that there was no other. I was out on the street, with heavy luggage to manage, in a strange town in the middle of the night. Oh, we suffer, we jet-propelled modern travellers, for all our developed world ... oh, and we tend to carry a little extra money in our pocket for these emergencies. I wonder if Joseph had any margin like that?

There was no way Joseph could have booked ahead. Our Saviour chose to be born in a backward place long before the telex, the phone and the fax. So when the caravan broke up on arrival in Main Street, Bethlehem, whatever vacant rooms remained in the town went to those who could move fast. Joseph couldn't, the way they were fixed. And listen, it's a terrible question, but did they even count themselves lucky, Joseph and Mary, when they found a stable vacant out the road?

Years ago, when the winds of change were blowing with special vigour in Holland, I was guest for a weekend in a big missionary house there. I quickly found that whatever else they might be throwing overboard, there was one traditional practice from which no deviations were tolerated. When the community gathered for its formal recreation hour, everybody, including the guest, was expected to be there. You could drink schnapps and smoke cigars if you liked, or abstain from either or both without harassment. You didn't have to converse if you preferred to be silent, and nobody asked you to sing or dance. But the unexpected small constraint, the having to be there with the household in its moment of relaxation, quickly gave you the feeling of being *family*. It was like being thrown a dishcloth and invited to help with the wash-up in anybody's kitchen!

There was no dishcloth for Mary or Joseph, or for their son, my Saviour. 'He came unto his own and his own received him not.' They did not even get a foot inside the door. Was it because John was so close to Mary and lived with her and knew her style with guests that this was so uppermost in his mind as he began to write his gospel?

There is a lovely story early in the Bible about Abraham receiving the messengers from God. Abraham fusses over them, sits them under a tree, begs them not to move, runs to the flock, picks a superior calf for their meal, shouts to Sarah to bake fresh bread, hurries with water to wash the guests' feet.

Don't think it doesn't happen any more. Welcome, and from the heart, is still big in the world: in countless homes, rich and poor, in ten thousand missions, in parishes, hospitals, farms, ranches, factories: wherever there are people of good will. And we can gather all the welcomes in all the world in all time into one and offer that, even now, to the timeless one who comes. For he comes to all of us, and he comes now.

Why not be a missionary?

Style

(January/February 1992)

Never in a thousand years would I want to own this thing. I'm sure of that. Not one smallest twinge of envy do I feel for the man or woman who does own it. But oh, my dear God (and I am saying a real prayer now), what a beauty we have here! And I am walking backwards right round about the car parked carelessly half across the driveway, practically singing songs of praise to the artist who designed it and the engineers who found a way to construct it and the workers and robots who finally put it together and painted and polished it. I can't take my eyes off its shining, red, low-slung, stretched-out gorgeousness. And I go my way praising the creator of all creators for the wonder and the beauty of – what you might call, but I hope you'd know better – just one more steel and rubber house on wheels.

It is a fun car, of course, and a luxury item, and for all I know it may be a big consumer of the earth's limited resources and a prodigal polluter of its ecology – but I love the look of it, and well I know that I would love the sound it makes – the rich deep thrum-m-m from the big silencers when it comes to life, the rising refined howl through the muffling baffles as the revs climb up the counter ... (oh, grow up!)

You're laughing at me, aren't you, car-worshipping at my age? But it's not just cars. It can be furniture, or a racehorse, or a humming-bird doing its helicopter act in front of a hibiscus flower; or nearly anything that seems perfect for the job it has to do. But there is maybe one other small extra thing that has to be there to give the sort of joyous satisfaction the red car gave me. I think I should call it – style.

I think if Our Lord had lived in today's world he might have illustrated his parables with stories about traffic lights, bingo, credit cards, or economy airfares. His rich young man might have arrived in a red sports car, and Jairus would surely have tried to get him on the phone about his dying daughter. It fascinates me that our Saviour chose for his own ministry of redemption a time when there were practically no mod cons, but then piled the media – the multimedia – into this corner of the second millennium when you and I just happen (oh yes?) to be here –

with our inescapable commission to make his story known. Figure it any way you like, it does sort of put the ball in our court, wouldn't you say?

Whatever we do with it, I'd hope we might do it with a bit of style. You remember the man in the parable who refused a wedding invitation with the implausible excuse that he had bought a new yoke of oxen and wanted to try them out. We should maybe show more understanding of this character's situation. Getting new oxen was probably like getting a new car. There are oxen – and then there are oxen. It was natural that he could not wait to make sure what he'd got.

You can be lucky and get that ox in a thousand, or that car in a thousand. You can fall on your feet and get your lifetime in this particular corner of the second millennium (call it this moment in a thousand) with the best news that ever was as your best kept secret, and the most marvellous ways and means and – say it! – *media* a Christian ever dreamed of there to hand for telling the world about it.

You may even be the person in a thousand with the vision to see precisely what you personally must do about it, and the will and ability to go and do it and – that rare extra thing that can sometimes enter in, whether it is cars or oxen or missionaries – to do it with style.

Why not be a missionary?

Consequences

(March 1992)

Any schoolboy or schoolgirl in the counties of Laois, Tipperary, Carlow or Kilkenny could tell you instantly what is the derivation of the placename *Borris*. I, however, have no idea, and on a Saturday morning in foreign parts, without the right kind of books and with nobody within reach to consult, I have a poor chance of finding out. I can still, nonetheless, use one of the several Borris-es I know about to direct the attentive reader to the starting point of this reflection, and if I cannot offhand foresee where that may lead us, this should merely give space to our setting out.

On the fine fast road, then, that runs east-ish out of Roscrea, you will come upon a village with the whimsically rhythmic name of Borris-in-Ossory. It is evidently so called to distinguish it from the quite unwhimsical town called simply Borris in the foothills of Mount Leinster, and from Borrisokane away to the west, Borrisoleigh to the south, and even from little Two-Mile-Borris which lies cheek-by-jowl with Moycarkey and Horse-and-Jockey in the other suburbs of the world-renowned sports-associated provincial city of Thurles.

A mere heartbeat after you have cleared Borris-in-Ossory, you select a pleasant little country road with signs steadily pointing (unless there has just been a big wind) to Ballacolla, Durrow, Kilkenny, Abbeyleix, and then you must keep your eyes open, not only for the tractors and articulated trucks that tend to bear down upon the unwary, but more especially for something of enormous significance which the signs unaccountably have failed to mention.

However well you have been prepared for it, the sudden appearance almost directly in your path of the great old abbey of Aghaboe takes you by surprise. It is somehow quite unexpected in this gentle unspectacular landscape among the green farms. Why did they site it here, you ask. No doubt they had their reasons and certainly any local schoolboy or schoolgirl could tell you what they were. What you do not need to ask is why people have taken such pains to preserve and restore the ruins, but you pause to give praise that the Board of Works and the AnCo workers have done it with such enlightened care and pride.

Why is Aghaboe significant, important and altogether wonderful? Surely because of what it stands for. And what does it stand for? Two things, principally, I think. More than twelve hundred years ago people were coming to dedicate their lives to God in this abbey, in the joyous scholarly austerity of an ancient Irish monastic community.

And the second reason? They were not closed in upon themselves in any cocoon-like existence. These good people had a vision relating to the far places, and a big generous care for the rest of the world. They felt irresistibly impelled to share their faith and learning with tribes and peoples far away. More than that: they had something driving them even to make missionaries out of those very peoples out there beyond the confines ...

It is part of the history of this abbey that its abbot, a scholar *of vast culture,* the books say, but specially qualified in mathematics and geography, resigned his post in the year 739, because he wanted to take off for the foreign missions. His name was Fergal, and he has been mentioned before on this page,* and he is still well remembered in the Austrian city of Salzburg where he ran another abbey and served as bishop and built a cathedral and trained missionaries and sent them out preaching and founding new communities, and no doubt pursued his own scientific studies, for about forty years, and eventually laid down his bones in 784.**

He was more or less three hundred years after Patrick, and here is an exciting thing: a priest I know who is familiar with the areas around Salzburg tells me that the people there, still to this day, have a lively devotion to St Brigid of Ireland. And where did that come from? You may well ask, and you may well answer: may it not have come with Fergal, perhaps, twelve hundred years ago, from the great abbey in the green fields just a stone's throw from Borris-in-Ossory?

Why not be a missionary?

---

* More than the music, page 171.
** Fergal was canonised in 1233 by Pope Gregory IX.

Sending signals

(May 1992)

When I go strolling with Mary the Mother of God, as I do most days, we say the Our Father together several times. The longer I live, the more central the Lord's Prayer becomes in my meagre devotions, because it really says everything for me that I want to say, and everything in it, the two – no the three – of us can and do say together. This thought can often stand me up: if Jesus and Mary, who are without needs or trespasses of their own, can ask with me – give *us* this day our daily bread ... forgive *us* our trespasses ... deliver *us* from evil ... well, that puts a whole new complexion on the incarnation. It brings them very close, gladly acknowledging their human roots, declaring their commitment to their *family, us*.

This is the way I get bogged down when I stroll with Mary the Mother of God. Yes, we say several Our Fathers, but what they cast up can spill over, so in between them Mary must have to listen, I think, with a lot of patience, to my fifty Hail Marys, and I sometimes think of her slipping the beads gently through her fingers, as Bernadette says she did with her that time back there at Massabielle, not so much to keep count, I suspect, as just to be companionable.

Well, she needs to be patient, because often enough the words I'm saying are just words, and my mind is really having a totally different kind of conversation with her; that's if it hasn't taken off on one of its free flights and become unconscious of her altogether! When that happens, I say to her, using a bit of one very sensible preface of the Mass: Well anyway, you have no need of my praise, and my prayers do nothing for you, how could they! But I do love being with you, just strolling like this, and what better background music could there be while my mind explores my deepest concerns of the moment with you than the ringing greeting to Gabriel, and the glad cry of Elizabeth and the confident shout of sinners who know they're safe once you're on their side?

Aha! Though! Let me tell you something about that Gabriel Archangel. It was because he made the great announcement that we call the Annunciation – something you are not going to forget, ever – that his name came up when the Church thought of appointing a heavenly Patron for Radio. Announcers are big in radio. So they appointed him, Gabriel, Patron of Radio. Now, I think anyone would agree that the said Gabriel, Archangel, owes you, heavenly Mother, and I think it's time you collected a little something on the debt.

I don't know how much clout a heavenly patron of anything has, but I think it must be a lot. And I wonder if you would consider suggesting in a delicate way to Gabriel that it's about time he knocked a few influential heads together in the Church, or maybe lit some fires under certain dragging feet, and got the great potential of radio properly activated in a few areas where a mighty radio job is waiting to be done for the gospel? There's one spot in particular you and I know, with three hundred acres of absolutely available land, located so strategically that it makes me dream desperately of big radio masts, and nobody is showing the slightest interest in doing anything, not to mention taking the slightest risk ... Let's see now, which *mystery* are we at? ... And what's Gabriel doing about it? I could even point him in a couple of directions where money might be found (the first thing everybody thinks of when they seek an objection that will excuse them from doing anything).

Let's say no more about this, dearest heavenly Mother, at least until our next stroll ... but you won't forget, will you, that the last day of this month of May (your month) this year is World Communications Day. There's such a lot yourself and Gabriel together could get moving by then.

Why not be a missionary?

The truth in love

(July/August 1992)

After Mass the young Sister came by the bench where I was unvesting. She stopped, waiting for me to look up, then: 'That was a fair disaster, wasn't it!' she said, in a kind of accusing tone, as if daring me to deny it. I made no pretence of not knowing what she was referring to. I made a kind of deprecating gesture, a combination of frown, shrug and toss of the head, dismissing the thing, and whispered with emphasis and solemnity, 'I understood every word,' then beamed at her. She gave me a hopeful-doubtful look and moved away slowly, considering it.

I thought what a variety of things there are which occasion suffering for good and decent people. Here was a case of someone very intelligent, unselfish, gentle and loving who somehow could not do a reading at Mass without stumbling over words, inverting phrases, and sounding nervous, uncertain and apologetic. It mattered so much to her, caused her such intense mortification. You could sense her cringing inside at the recollection of her latest blunders. This was no joke and ought not to be treated lightly ...

I called quietly to her and when she turned said, 'You are probably the only one who remembers – or cares – that you weren't quite BBC class this morning. Anyway this is not a broadcasting station.' (The idea made her laugh.) 'You're very brave to go up there in your turn to read before them all when you know you don't have to. You'll be a lot better the next time, when you've got over your stage fright. Anyway, do you think you're going to be judged in the end on how well you read?' She knew the answer to this one. 'Well, on what then?' She had a ready answer to that one too: To act justly, to love tenderly, to walk humbly, *et cetera* ... 'So go and do that, will you, and offer it up for me!' I think she felt better. It was the best I could do early in the morning.

There was an old friend who came by later in the day, passing from an assignment where he had just spent several of his best years to another where there was little so far in prospect but change and challenge. He was still only partly disengaged and kept reverting to concerns which really should be no longer his.

At the same time, he had all kinds of plans for dealing with the insecurities of the still unknown future and needed to kick them around and get reactions. Well, if you were really going to be all things to all men, and if what this man needed quite badly was a sounding board, you had to try to be it. So *listen and react* became part of the day's programme.

There were other bits and pieces: a heartbreaking wonderful story by two parents, in a foreign magazine, the life story of the handicapped little son who was everything in the world to them for all of his six years, and how they found a way of coping with his death. They had words better than any I could ever think of to comfort two friends of mine just recently devastated by the death of their little handicapped daughter. Translations take work and time, so ... there had to be a session with a dictionary and typewriter in between times, and there would have to be others to finish the job.

What's all this to do with being a missionary? Well, really, that's nearly all there is to it! Every day is a day when we have to fit a lot of things (words, doings, listenings, waitings) in between a lot of other things following one simple rule of thumb. The rule of thumb is that people must always get priority. And sometimes you remember Moses asking God: How did I get into this? How did I get responsible for all these people? Did I bring them into the world? But you're glad, like Moses, to be doing what you are doing.

Why not be a missionary?

For ever and a dream

(September/October 1992)

Nineteen fifty-two, nineteen ninety-two, and quite suddenly it is forty years. So at once, the idea of a favourite pursuit springs to mind: celebration! Still, what is a fortieth anniversary, really? Just another whistle stop on a fairly long journey, might you not say? And the train goes on ... the trouble is, though, someone has to decide where the train goes next. And so, well, for pity's sake, here we go again ...

To clarify: this is the fortieth October in a row in which it has fallen to the hapless lot of the same reluctant author to provide material to fill this page. And where do we go from here?

Can we just maybe stay with trains? If you have ever gone down out of Austria through the Brenner Pass into Italy, you must certainly have noticed that the pass has a lot more to it than the town of Brennero on the border, and a customs post where the articulated trucks of half Europe line up night and day waiting their turn to cross north or south. No, the pass through those mighty mountains reached surely from Innsbruck, already deep in Austria, right down through the length of the South Tyrol and on practically to the city of Verona. Just short of that city, the hills fall back on either side, and quite dramatically, the horizons open on a vast agricultural plain which will seem to stretch on for ever with not the smallest ripple of a hill ...

'Does the road wind uphill all the way?' enquired some long ago poet, and solemnly answered his own question: Yes, to the very end. Rubbish, says I – anyway, if you are referring to this journey. Oh yes, there is a lot of climbing, and usually more to be expected along the way, but why should the level stretches be denied, or the long gradients where coasting is pure joy? If there is one thing more than another this world can do without, it is pious humbug about the priesthood. And yes, of course, I am talking abut the priesthood. You did not really think this page is more than very marginally concerned with railways or geography, did you?

The priesthood – when you've been there for a long time you can say with some authority, even with some credibility, what it's been like. If you haven't been there, you can only guess or theorise, and there's where the humbug often begins. A lot of the climbing, struggle, pushing yourself, and holding yourself back, comes when you're young enough to deal with it, when your energy and optimism are unblunted. Hardly knowing it, you develop your own style, see your own visions, oh – and dream your own dreams. Your eyes search the hills and find ways through, and often you even opt for ways that are not the easiest, because the heights actually challenge you. One thing, nobody ever, ever, blinkers you. Special pains are taken, in fact, to show you the chasms and the hazards. If you still go on, that is your decision, and you will stand over it.

So maybe you come through all this stronger, probably wiser, with some sort of balance already achieved, enough maturity attained in the only way maturity can ever be attained, so that you are half ready for the horizons when the hills fall back, and the plain where most of your days are going to be spent opens before you, broad enough, heaven knows, to absorb all the forces of your best working years.

But, who is to say when you will reach your best? If you keep the dream intact and a few of the stars still in your eyes, you will never, ever, have any doubt that the best is yet to come. You'll keep climbing out of the ruts of routine that are one of the most insidious hazards, and you will keep yourself open to what is new: ideas, methods, insights, ways of getting into hearts and turning the world round ... with an old and very wonderful message that does not change. Something like this was the thought of that sound man St Paul, 'forgetting what lies behind and straining forward to what lies ahead, I press on towards the goal ...' Reaching the goal would be a lot of fun!

Why not be a missionary?

The high ground

(November 1993)

Sometimes there are hundreds of people with me, and other times there may be a mere two or three. Sometimes, again, there is nobody but myself, and when that happens I just pause a small moment at the beginning and quite deliberately gather the whole world around me, the inner circle of my family and close friends, the suffering and terrorised and all who are in great need and the whole great beloved messy mixed-up human race of men and women, Christian, Muslim, Jewish, non-believers, atheists, agnostics, the lot. For what is now to be done concerns them all, whether they know it or not, whether they believe it or not. Some, I know, who did once believe, now no longer believe (or think they don't), and these are gathered with the rest, for the purpose-built assembly here taking shape is not in the business of judging, rejecting, condemning or excluding; it is solely for the purpose of reaching out, of reconciling, of healing, saving, gathering in, embracing, loving, making one, making good, making happy ...

We begin very contritely, knowing so intensely the poverty of the response our lives have given to the love of a gracious Father who made us and has kept us to this day drawing breath. We listen in our distracted, half-attentive way as he speaks to us in the readings, and we ask him to re-make our minds to think as he thinks, our hearts to feel and to love as he does. And then we brace ourselves for what is to follow.

What follows is a story which is more than a story, and it begins, variously: 'On the night he was betrayed ...' or 'The day before he suffered ...' or 'When the time came for him to be glorified by you, his heavenly Father ...' And I am there before all the world, the believing and the unbelieving, and I am holding the bread in my hands and saying the words that Jesus said, aloud, for all the world to hear ... and holding the cup of wine and saying his words over it and lifting it up for all the world to see ... and I am telling the assembly that he, that Jesus, said: 'Do this ...'

What I have just done is exactly what he, what Jesus, asked should be done *in memory of him*. Was it solely for this that I became a priest? No. But it was one of the reasons, by itself, to make me choose the priesthood again, and again, and again as my life. Every time I stand at an altar and do what I have just done, I am really, and I suppose fairly consciously, affirming that what I chose once I choose now again, and forever. Maybe what I chose was just to be chosen, for I remember that Jesus said: 'You have not chosen me; I have chosen you, and have sent you ...' If that was it, then that is what I choose again.

But there is more. Standing here, alone in a sense before the world, I am making another affirmation, a public profession of something I believe with all my being. This on the table between us that appears to be bread is no longer bread. This that was wine is not wine. Here between us lies the body of Christ, really and truly. Here is his blood, his soul and divinity. Here is the Lamb of God who takes away the sin of the world, and yours and mine. Here is food and drink come down from heaven, to make us grow and render us strong, to make us live with God's very own life, to make us one, as Jesus here planned and prayed, one with the Father, and with himself, and one in closest unity, closest union, tightest-knit community ... with one another.

Why not be a missionary?

Irregular acquaintances

(June 1994)

The little boy was a hefty eighteen-month-old, already quite steady on his feet, and with energy to burn. He was going to be around for a while, so I thought I'd better develop a manageable personal relationship with him early on. I risked touching him with a finger on the very tip of his nose when he wasn't looking, and he caught on instantly that this was a new game, and entered into it gladly. He began to weave, challenging me with his eyes, laughing uproariously when I got through the defences. I knew then that I was going to like him, but that I must change the game before I accidentally bled his nose. I remembered the very thin Alsatian I met in a garden centre the previous day. He had a stone in his mouth and he kept on pushing against me, then dropping the stone at my feet and challenging me to grab it before he could. I knew I could lose a hand that way, all in fun, but I hated to disappoint the dog. How, I wondered, did I so frequently get myself into silly situations like this ...

The boy's parents were gentle people, very devoted to him and to each other. They were friends of friends, and I knew practically nothing about them, except that somebody had mentioned in passing that they were *living together*. It became plain they assumed I knew this. In the course of the few hours we spent together, other bits and pieces of information were volunteered. Another baby was on the way, and evidently much looked forward to. In the background somewhere was an older child of one or the other, this one also evidently much loved by both. When we meet again, as we probably shall, other pieces of the story may be revealed, some of the whys and wherefores of their situation, what prospects there may be of regularising it, even whether they feel any need to regularise it. For the moment, I take nothing at all for granted, and I carefully make no judgements. I do remember to pray for these new acquaintances, and I wonder idly what formula or euphemism I might have used if I had had to introduce them to anyone else.

Now, why do I tell you all this? Well, I suppose, to give you a practical illustration of the kind of thing currently happening in my life as a priest/missionary. It is what this column has always tried to do. I cannot give you the whole story in one short piece, so I give you one vignette at a time. You piece the bits together over a period, and maybe you get some idea what a priest/ missionary is/ does/ thinks/ feels/ endures/ enjoys/ deplores/ or whatever, in his contact with daily realities.

Casual social contact with people in situations like that of my new friends is a relatively new reality for me, but I've got to learn fast to be at ease with it. A growing number of my acquaintances – and a close friend or two among them – have been *moving in* with chosen companions without benefit of ceremony or sacrament. Mostly, there is no attempt at concealment, nor is there much evidence of guilt feelings or any great sense of culpability. No two cases are quite the same, of course, but in all instances they have their reasons, or think they have, or want to think they have. Who am I to say, unless they tell me all about it, and that, generally, they don't – why should they?

But in the rare instance where they do, my concern must surely be to give them a totally honest reaction, though always with calm and courtesy. If they are surprised, shocked or angry (and indeed that happens) that I indicate less than complete approval for the state of things and insist that considerations of right and wrong may have to limit the exercise of their adult human freedom, there is only left to say, gently and firmly: 'Come off it! There is not one law for you and a different law for me, we share the same faith and the same obligations.'

The nice thing is that I am not called upon to judge my neighbour, to declare him a sinner, or to write him off as ready for irrevocable condemnation. I cannot see to the depths of the heart as God does, and anyway, whatever he may see there, I am certainly not allowed to set limits to his patience. I keep a picture in my mind of a self-righteous crowd with stones in their hands all ready to throw, while Christ quietly draws patterns in the sand – and waits them out.

Why not be a missionary?

To nail it down

(July/August 1994)

It was a very big church with a lot of side chapels, and a lot of tourists who seemed more interested in architecture than in religion were milling around with guides, talking out loud. I managed anyway to find a confessional, with a man inside who spoke my language, and I brought myself and him up to date on the current situation inside me. He talked good sense to me, and at the end gave me the sort of penance I find very difficult to do even reasonably well. He asked me to say the Our Father seven times, in honour of something or other (I now forget what). I took myself off with great goodwill to the side chapel where the Blessed Sacrament was exposed in a simple, plain monstrance for adoration, and found it full of very devout people, both young and old, all clearly immersed in prayer. The least I could do was try to get into the mood, so I knelt down and lifted my eyes to the host, and tried to tune in.

Have you ever attempted to say seven Our Fathers one after the other, and make them mean what they are supposed to mean? Well, this time I had one circumstance going for me. The gospel that morning had been about the apostle Philip saying to Jesus: 'You just show us the Father and we shall be satisfied!' I once more, as always happens when I read that passage, felt the same astonishment as Philip must have at the reply. 'It can't be possible, Philip, that after all this time, you still do not know me. Surely you realise that when you see me, you are looking at the Father? That he is in me and I am in him? Surely it is obvious that the things I have been doing are *his* doing?'

And there was I suddenly – appallingly – looking at the host in the simple circular frame, over the heads of the nun-adorers-on-duty in their quaint choir-cloaks, and over the heads of the surprisingly devout tourists, for that moment totally understanding that I was looking into the Father's face. My seven Our Fathers began spontaneously, and for once I stayed with them to the end without a single deviation. Too soon, they were over, but there was nowhere I wanted to go. The moment of grace when you have the Father all to yourself – it doesn't strike that often. When it does, you want to stay with it, stretch it out.

I stretched this moment out, reflecting that – isn't there a lot of *movement*, of comings and goings, in God's dealings with us men and women in this world? God so loved the world that *he sent* his only son to save us. The son came, to save, not to judge, to bring life, to destroy death. There came a day when he said: 'You are sad because I've told you: I am *going away*, and you cannot come with me now; but really it is to your advantage that I go, because I am going to *send* the Advocate to you from my Father.' So he goes, *ascends*, to the Father, and next thing you know, it is Pentecost, and the Holy Spirit comes, *descends*, to stay with us for ever, to bring back to our minds everything that Jesus has taught us, to guide and illumine and sanctify and take care of us as long as we are here.

But that, I almost said out loud, is not the end of the comings and goings. What about that other promise Jesus made: 'When someone loves me he will keep my word, and my Father will love him, and *we will come to him* and make our abode with him?' So I can go out now and get on with my day's work – and be sure that Father, Son and Holy Spirit have not stayed behind here in this very peaceful chapel, and left me to go on my own.

And then I remember, almost as if it were something new and strange, what my day's work – every day – is concerned with, and then – not content with having got my seven Our Fathers safely (even devoutly!) said, I launch into yet another. I want to *nail* this down. What my day's work – every day – is concerned with is the construction of something called *the reign of God* in my community, in my neighbourhood, in the world, anywhere I can reach. You may prefer, as I do, to call it by its old name, *the kingdom*. But whatever we call it, it will only come to be with a bit of *outside* help (which now, in our new enlightenment, we know must come from *inside* of you and me – where God has taken up his abode, don't you see!). Which explains my eighth Our Father, because, like all the others, it asks that the kingdom may come.

Why not be a missionary?

The insiders

(September/October 1994)

The lights went from green to amber, but there were just too many of us to sneak through before the red. We lurched to a reluctant halt with our noses to the line and nothing to spare. This was the moment he chose, when we were trapped helplessly for the next three minutes of our lives by the gadgets of modern living, to come at us with his disarming grin, brandishing in his upraised hand a T-shaped instrument for cleaning windscreens. He was young. He was handsome. He might have been Latin American, or North African, or Middle Eastern. Or he could have been East European. At any rate, we were his heaven-sent target, and he had maybe two minutes to make a killing. Meanwhile, a whole squad of his mates, similarly armed, fanned out through the stalled traffic.

Their very numbers make this a little intimidating, but there is seldom any danger from the itinerant salesmen; and their good-humoured pressure tactics are no more than a normal hazard of the road. All over Europe, and in many other regions of the earth, the marginalised, the immigrants, legal and illegal, the gypsy youth, impecunious students, the unemployed, the opportunists, are scratching some sort of precarious living offering small services at traffic lights. Wash your windscreen, sell you flowers, contraband cigarette-lighters, air-fresheners, paper handkerchiefs, or novelties. They always call you *boss*, which makes you feel you're being got at! Anyway, you either accept what they are offering (whether you need it or not) and give them some small recompense, or you reject them, wave them off, say your boorish *no* (maybe with exasperated embellishments) – and drive away feeling bad about it ... you have so much, they have so little ... yes, but ... and you try to rationalise your bad temper ... they are a dangerous distraction in traffic, a nuisance, perhaps a menace ... you have no money you can reach because of your seat belt ... you have no small change anyway ... the authorities should do something ...

You learn a lot about yourself at traffic lights in the cities of the nineties. With this new kind of *third world* on your doorstep you find yourself reflecting that you, for no reason of your deserving, are on the inside of a privileged circle, from which very many are excluded. Even if you never felt privileged before, there is no way you can any longer escape the experience – and it is not at all a pleasant experience, because somehow it comes with guilt and self-reproach attached. And despite all you may have heard and read about communal guilt and structural injustice, you really cannot see that you are personally responsible for all the world's upheavals. But you do know you are feeling a new kind of uneasiness, and that something has to be done about it. Something, that is, which goes far beyond making small handouts in response to emotional blackmail. Something other than mere adjustments in your lifestyle that might make the difference between you and the hordes of young men at the traffic lights less obvious. Well, what, then?

It has got to be something to do with *the kingdom* – you become more and more certain of that. The kingdom of God, the reign of God, the group in any place or time that constitutes Christ's genuine serious followers. Christ's people: this is another circle you know you belong to, and want to belong to. And here there is no guilty feeling of excluding others, because you want and want desperately that everybody without exception should belong.

Oh, grand, then! So you only have to go and evangelise at the traffic lights of the world? Not that; it sounds simple, but it would be quite impossible, for every time the lights change, the manpower simply rushes to the other arm of the crossing to get their three minutes' worth against the competition. This is no captive audience on a quiet hillside.

So, probably, nearly all you can do is to make the kingdom a very vibrant reality, make it really live, so that it can, must, attract ... *all the outsiders* ... and make them feel at home and wanted. That means, of course, that you go to work *on yourself*, first, and all the time, according to the well-publicised formulae. What formulae? How about some of these: keeping the commandments, even the least ones, is recommended in order to be the greatest in the kingdom; living the beatitudes (poor in spirit, gentle, merciful, compassionate, concerned about justice for all) guarantees a list of appropriate and very specific benefits; treating others as you'd wish them to treat you: loving your neighbour as yourself, loading up with the gifts and fruits of the Holy Spirit. It's only a beginning, but it's the best *beginning* you can make when you go fixing the world's problems.

Why not be a missionary?

High hearts

(November 1994)

The garbage truck, with its built-in mill for reducing everything to powder, just happens recently to set up for work right beneath the chapel window at the precise moment when the homily is beginning. I promised a visitor one morning that the nuisance would abate in a few minutes, but that was the morning a big yellow machine moved in on the heels of the departing garbage truck to excoriate the road in preparation for resurfacing. It got me reflecting on my lifetime experience with sacraments and sacred moments of all kinds. The environment, in fact, in which I have had to carry out my ministry has rarely, very rarely, been in the least conducive to flights of mystic ecstasy – let alone a minimum of devotion.

I say to myself: 'Well, I'm not here to wallow in spiritual consolation; I'm not doing what I am doing so that I may feel stroked and cherished by the Holy Spirit; it's no part of the contract that I should *feel* closer to God, or feel anything, when I do what I was ordained to do.' Which is all fine and dandy, but ...

I baptised a niece's baby once. She had astonishingly powerful lungs and she yelled her way through the ceremony with such single-minded dedication that nobody, including myself, heard a word I said. She was not a nasty-minded baby, then or later, I must add; it was just that she was *starving*. Her mother later smilingly confessed that she had forgotten to feed her little one that morning in all the excitement of preparing for the ceremony.

Another baptism – oh dear – and a long time ago. It started out as a sick call to a woman who had just given birth. Coming in from bright light, I had trouble finding her in the total darkness of a small hut. To my surprise – because I am not normally very squeamish – I was staggering when I came out, but it happened I was coming down with German measles and did not know it. The catechist gave me a funny look, and in his tactful way suggested that, 'Father might perhaps wish to baptise the baby.' I hadn't thought of the baby, and certainly hadn't seen him, or been aware of his presence. We found him, though, and even if the conditions were not exactly perfect for the ceremony, the water was poured and the words were said, and a little boy was born again, and it was a magic moment in spite of all. And I finished in hospital that same day, covered with spots!

What are you supposed to do when you cannot *get at* the patient, to whom you are supposed to administer the last rites? No, I'm serious, you do meet situations about which there is nothing in the books or training courses. For instance, you find the soles of the patient's feet meeting you right in the doorway, and the bed is precisely the full of the room, and short of climbing on it, there is no way you can get in, and nowhere else to stand or sit or otherwise place yourself, even if you do. Common sense and desperation will find solutions to practical problems of this kind, but you can wave goodbye to feelings of devotion.

Oh well, we live in a pretty disorderly world, and we are a very messy human race, and it helps a great deal to remember that we carry our most precious treasures in earthen vessels. Even if I feel rugged enough, I remember I am a fragile, vulnerable, fallible, very mortal human being, and no better than my neighbours. I don't need a rucksack, or a thing, in order to carry my stock in trade. What I've got, and – more important – what I've got to give, for the most part, I can carry within me. Was this, I wonder, what Jesus was teaching his disciples when he told them to travel light, with no satchel or shoe or money in their purses?

All that need concern you, he was saying to them, is that your stock in trade is life-giving, strengthening, healing, reconciling, fortifying, saving. You can safely stand most deprivations. You will learn to put up, even gladly, with all the mess.

Why not be a missionary?

The narrow gate

(January/February 1995)

He walked upright and confidently, with an unselfconscious swing to his body that told you he was his own man. He was young, bearded, ragged, with things hanging out of him. He had some kind of plastic bag for a shoulderpack. He might be a tramp, or a late-flourishing hippie, or even (and probably) what my African friends would have called a crazeman. The description is imprecise because I did not have time or leisure to observe the details attentively. He came unexpectedly into my view as I rounded a slow curve on the motorway at speed. He was jaywalking across my path and only a couple of hundred yards away. He gave no impression of being angry or hostile or of making any kind of protest. He was a man intent on crossing the road, at his own pace, after his own fashion, minding his own business. But he suddenly became my business, because I had to find, very quickly, a way of saving his life, without causing a pile-up of the fast coming traffic that half my mind was watching in the rear mirrors.

We slowed, all of us, to a virtual halt, and the danger passed. But what stayed with me was the powerful feeling of protectiveness generated by the moment. This unknown man's life was suddenly in our keeping. We might – and with reason – have been furious with him, but instead, I think, we found something very like love drawing circles around him. We found everything in us *willing* to stave off the danger he was in.

I think I know (though I'm not sure anybody else will) why this little experience ties up in my mind with a story from the missions that a colleague told me. Parish councils, he explained, can sometimes be severe on the erring ones in the flock, and will blow the whistle with some alacrity on public impropriety, particularly if it has to do with sexual mores or marital irregularity. What his parish council came to him about, however, was something a little different. They demanded that he should deny Holy Communion to two people in the community who were *not speaking* to each other. This was scandalous conduct, they felt, which should not be tolerated among *kingdom people.*

Here at the gateway to a very new year, do I hear you reflecting that the parish council was right in its drastic demand? Well, let's think for a moment about gateways. Our Lord mentioned one, a narrow one! People asked him: 'Are there many who will be saved?' and, instead of answering the question directly, he told them, 'Strive to enter by the narrow gate.' There was a fine broad road running to perdition, he said, and lots of people tended to choose that way. They shouldn't. And we shouldn't. Well we know it.

Consider, though. Our Lord warned us the gate was narrow. He never did suggest that it was *too* narrow to let me, or you, or anyone, through. That must be our first thought this new year. The narrow gate is wide open to me. Well, fine, fine, fine – but how do I line up for it? We are told, 'If you want to enter into life, keep the commandments.' We are told what the greatest commandments are, the two that sum up all the law and all the prophets. Love God, that is the first. Love the neighbour, that is the second. The second can sometimes seem harder than the first, but it is no less vital. The parish council understood this. No use offering your gift at the altar till you've got reconciled with your brother, or your sister. The gate is too narrow, it seems, for those who will not forgive. It is too narrow for me, or for you, only if we will not love.

On last All Saints Day I listened to a gentle old bishop preaching at a Mass in a golden lovely cathedral. He talked about the mighty numbers of our ancestors and contemporaries who even now enjoy the vision of God in heaven. He was very sure of one thing. It would be *an absurdity* if the vast bulk of the human race lovingly created by God, and for whom he gave his only Son, came to be excluded in the end from the enjoyment of his love in glory. A total *absurdity*, he declared. Narrow gate or no narrow gate, he was certain any of us could squeeze in. Are you not certain he was right? And that we can help our neighbour to squeeze in too? You should be. Happy New Year!

Why not be a missionary?

A matter of principle

(April 1995)

A farming man told me a great story, and there was a sort of awed wonder in his voice, and there was pride in his eyes. Coming home from an outing round about Christmas, he found the sort of devastation that farmers have nightmares about. He found his flock of sheep in disarray, and several of them lying dead. He knew there had been a visitation from a pack of dogs in his absence. He knew that, with most of the dead ewes carrying lambs, and many of the survivors certain to have problems at lambing time after this day's crushing and panicking, his losses in financial terms were hardly to be thought about.

Every so often, usually near Christmas, some television station gives a re-run of a great old film, called, I think, *Far from the Madding Crowd*. It so happened that I had watched a bit of one of those re-runs a few days back, and what had stayed with me was a terrible scene in which a trusted collie unaccountably turned rogue, betrayed his trust, and during the night while his master was sleeping, set about worrying the large flock in the sheepfold and caused them to break out on to the Downs and fling themselves down a steep slope into the sea. In the next scene, the now bankrupt owner was setting out with a pack on his back to look for a job as someone else's shepherd.

I had a fairly accurate picture, then, of what my friend was talking about, but he did not linger over the details of the massacre. He wanted to get on to the next scene, and he sketched it simply, with no drama at all. Just with awe and wonder and a great deal of pride. A man with whom he was casually friendly, the owner of a neighbouring farm not far away, came to him a day or two after the disaster. He said: 'I have to tell you it was my dogs did this job on your sheep. I'll have to make it up to you as best I can. One thing I could not do would be to look you in the face for the rest of our lives without having told you and settled the damage.'

I believe the man who told me the story was actually awed by a new awareness of what he knew perfectly well already, namely, that there were people of the greatest integrity among his everyday acquaintances. He was quite evidently very proud to find one of his own breed so thoroughly upright and honourable. Something else, too, was clearly dawning on him after days of reflection on the events he was recounting. He would have done the same himself had the positions been reversed. It was a side of himself he had never known about before, but it felt surprisingly good.

When and if you read this, it will be deep in Lent, with Easter coming very close. Should I have talked to you perhaps about big issues like human rights, structural injustice, abuse of the weak and innocent, or some other of the huge and awful crimes humanity perpetrates and is victim to? No, I don't think so at all. Communal guilt is easy enough to live with. And who appointed you or me to issue blanket condemnations, anyway? But think of the decent man with the trusted dogs that turned rogue, and you've really got something useful to chew on.

Think of a *yes* which always means *yes,* and of a personal word that can be relied upon, absolutely and always. Your *yes,* your *no,* your word. Here we are really into the nitty gritty ... getting so very close to the essential you. A you incapable of even a small falsehood – if *any* lie can be called small. The you you'd certainly want to be, but probably are already. Truth, sincerity, integrity, straight dealing – with these things alone you, we, all of us, can start now turning the world around.

Honesty, I suppose, is the reverse of greed, or anyway, a very good cure for it. Any thing in the world, from the crown jewels to a mere tube of toothpaste, either belongs to me or doesn't. What doesn't, I keep my hands off. Elementary, isn't it? It is what faith, parents, even the laws of God and humanity, have always told me. So ... let you, I, all of us, act accordingly and certainly the world turns around. We teach these simple things by word and example; yes, it certainly turns around.

Why not be a missionary?

Pointing fingers and stiffening spines

(June 1995)

'They're looking up at you and you can actually see in their eyes when they switch off ...' So said a good woman from Dublin, who does the readings regularly in her parish church. She was complaining about 'whoever put that lectionary together'. To her mind, they put in too many pieces full of placenames and people's names which were just plain unpronounceable. Nabuchadnezzar, for instance; *who* has the stomach for listening to a reader stumbling over a name like that at seven in the morning!

All very well, I suggested, but if you won't have Nabuchadnezzar, you'll have to do without Shadrach, Meshach and Abednego, and you'll miss the thrill and inspiration of their great fighting response to the bloodcurdling threats of the aforesaid unpronounceable N. You'll throw away a great opportunity for stiffening the Christian spines of your Mass-goers.

Just listen to those brave boys, S, M and A: 'If our God is able to save us from the whitehot fiery furnace and from your power, O king, he will save us; and even if he does not, then you must know *(anyway)*, O king, that we will not serve your god or worship the statue you have erected.' And that's telling him!

It is no harm at all, I think, to hit us every now and then with those old Bible stories of black and white badness and goodness, of vicious criminality and unassailable integrity, of straightforward right and wrong. The chaste Susanna came up again a while back in the readings of Lent, fresh and good and lovely as ever, and still badly done by. She was under false accusation by two corrupt judges, vindictive old men smarting under the humiliation after she rejected their lustful advances. The assembly believed the malicious lie they told (because after all they were who they were) and promptly condemned her to stoning, apparently without hearing her version of the story. One fellow in the crowd was having none of it, though; *a boy named Daniel*. Daniel stood up to be counted, and his cry was: *Count me out!* A forceful boy he must have been, because we quickly find them all back having a re-trial and Susanna is exonerated, and the two old scoundrels are getting their just deserts, in other words, a good decisive stoning. And so, in a manner of speaking, all ends happily!

Is it the Christophers or who that use for a slogan: *You can make a difference?* It's a good slogan for any and every wilting Christian in our day. Okay we have to take our share of the fall-out when one of us, or indeed more of us, lets down the side and shames us all and falls from whatever pedestal he/she is on (and the higher it is the farther the fall for him or her, and the denser the flak for us). Okay we hang our heads and cringe – and, if we have sense, acknowledge that *but for the grace of God there goeth Philip* – it could have been me, dammit, in similar circumstances, and well I know it, and who am I to point a finger! And who are *you* to point a finger, either, my fellow sinner!

But I *can* still and all make a difference, can't I? You could say I'm *pro-choice*, even, but in this sense, that I know right from wrong, and the choice between the one and the other is mine to make, and nobody is taking that away from me. That's what personal freedom means, isn't it? – and am I not personally free? I don't have to go with any particular trend I dislike or disagree with, and I can swim against any stream if I don't like its direction, and I can say *yes* and I can say *no* and make it stick, and *I'm* the one to decide whether *I'm* going to be a man or a mouse.

I can carry the choice high above and far beyond the mere minimum of choosing right above wrong, too. I can choose better above good and best above better. I can carry the war against evil into the camp of the enemy, and wipe out the bad by sheer force of the good I do. I can, so to speak, go the whole hog, and turn my entire life into a personal crusade – to turn the world around. I can even – and why not? – well, why not be a missionary?

Heading out:
Is there a specifically missionary *thing*?

(July/August 1995)

One of the most haunting sounds in the world, I think, is the three farewell blasts you hear on a ship's siren as she leaves port. It is a sound which brings me back to Liverpool, and to a winter's night a lot of years ago when the battered old ship I travelled on to my first missionary posting pulled away from the Prince's Wharf, and we were at last on our way. We watched the lights going down behind us, and somewhere a long way clear of the harbour the pilot boat drew alongside to take off the pilot, and there went our last link with land. It was all so romantic and in its way thrilling, and we went down to our narrow tiered bunks in the little steel-walled cabins feeling wonderful, and soon fell asleep in a kind of emotional exhaustion. This was the life.

In the morning we woke up to a great silence. There was no sound of engines, and no sensation of moving. We found we were back in Liverpool, tied up once more at a wharf. We had sprung a leak during the night, and it was a big enough leak to have forced a prudent return to harbour. And there we spent many more days while they fixed the damage, and they must have fixed it well, because we were later tossed about the Bay of Biscay in a tremendous storm for two or three days, and tremendous quantities of the ship's crockery were smashed, and not many cared, because, in the misery of seasickness they never expected to eat again. But we made it to the calmer waters of the Canaries, and saw the schools of dolphins playing and the shoals of flying fishes pretending they were birds, and felt the beginnings of tropical heat, and prayed for the captain to change into whites, because ship's etiquette prescribed that we couldn't until he did!

I remember climbing to the bridge at night to watch Las Palmas on the radar as we passed nearby, (oh, and you can't imagine what a new thing radar was then, or the marvel of that sweep hand lighting up the coast on the dim green dial). There was, then, the excitement of seeing land after many days at sea. There was Cape Verde first, and a quick visit to Bathurst, now Banjul, to drop passengers and cargo. I remember the whole business of *coaling* in a harbour in Sierra Leone, so I suppose we must have been steam-powered. The old ship, I should have said, was on her last voyage, and was going back home to be broken up.

I remember the geography we learned, the quaintly-named Pepper Coast (which must have been Liberia), and Cape Palmas where we made another sighting, and the Ivory Coast (which has remained the Ivory Coast to this day, except that now they say it in French, Côte d'Ivoire) and the Gold Coast (now Ghana) and we stood off Accra and dropped alighting passengers by bosun's chair into canoes tossing on the surf. And we made harbour in a place with the lovely name, Takoradi, where I think we *coaled* again, and it was no more than a day or two from there to Lagos, and there we disembarked, and set off overland, nine of us on the back of a lorry, two more days and nights, and were spilled out eventually on the bank of the Niger River, to make our way by canoe, etc. etc. etc. Am I boring you?

I saw a very enchanting thing on a blustery September day a year or two ago. I was standing on a rock on the coast somewhere near Spiddal, and down the middle of that long stretch of bay between Galway City and the open Atlantic there went, leaping and diving in highest good humour, a large school of dolphins. I really don't know why this experience was so moving and beautiful, but I think it may have been because they were *heading out*, leaving the security of the bay behind them, and making for the open sea and for whatever unknown risks or ecstasies might happen to await them there. I found the missionary in me somehow responding to those gentle creatures setting out on their brave adventure, just as it does invariably to the farewell triple-blast of a ship's siren, or to the sight of a plane's wheels *unsticking* as it heads for the far places.

Is there, you may ask, a specifically missionary *thing* that drives and urges otherwise fairly normal men and women away out from their anchors and securities, and leaves them somehow uneasy and out of sorts unless they keep the far places and the far people and the far-fetched job they feel compelled to undertake as the focus of their lives? I don't know how to answer, but maybe missionaries do it better than they talk about it. What I do know is that for months after every Easter Season, I am haunted by the thought of twelve very human apostles, and the job they were left with, and how *far* each of them went to do it.

Why not be a missionary?

Mission accomplished

(November 1995)

St Patrick's, Kiltegan, I remember, was not yet into its twenties when it occurred to one of the still rather young folk responsible for planning its future that some sort of provision had better be made for burying the Society's dead – whenever it might chance to have dead to bury. There was some discussion, and I think a bit of testing of the ground here and there, before the choice of a suitable place was eventually made, and as soon as that was settled, they railed in – and later *walled* in – a burial place at the very highest point on the property. With the possible exception of one on the Hill of Slane, I do not know any cemetery anywhere with a finer view! While this may be of little concern to the occupants – and what view could possibly compare with the beatific vision they are, we pray, enjoying? – it does make their resting place a very attractive place to visit.

It is much visited. Coming in from foreign parts, or from anywhere, near or far, whether the absence has been long or short, you have hardly greeted the living and claimed a place to spend the night when you find the urge in you to climb the hill and have a bit of a wander around among the dead. There are by this time two quite long rows of little stone crosses giving names and dates, and another two rows much shorter, but growing steadily. These mark the graves of any who were at home or within reach when their moment came. Limestone slabs on a wall nearby list the names of all members who are buried elsewhere around the globe, with the relevant dates and the names of their missions. So the tally is complete, as far as it goes.

The rows and lists will grow, certainly, inevitably, inescapably. That is not something you worry about. Your own moment will come, of course you know, so naturally you intend (and pray!) to be found *watching* when it does, for 'blessed are those servants who are found watching ...' Beyond that, you make no plans, and nourish no particular concern.

You never think of picking a favourite place here. You never tell yourself that it is in this companionable spot, in this congenial company, that you wish to take your last rest. To think like that would be a sort of betrayal of what you are. A missionary stays loose, ready to set out tomorrow, today if necessary, for any place in the world where he is sent. The earth is all God's, and any six feet of it will serve as well as any other for a resting place when the tools finally fall from his hands. And this is his freedom.

But there is no smallest danger you will forget any of the old friends, colleagues, partners, fellow-travellers, companions in many a venture – and adventure, brothers one and all, whose bones are buried, or names inscribed on stone, here on this hill. There is not even any real feeling of separation from them, for in the Communion of Saints access is never totally denied, and *life is but changed, not taken away*. Militant, suffering, and triumphant, this family of missionaries remains a unit, stays together, struggles on with St Patrick, and with its extended family of parents, relatives, friends and benefactors, till its mission is accomplished. And so, as Paul wrote so confidently to his Thessalonians, 'We shall always be with the Lord,' and so again, as he added: 'Comfort one another with these words.'

Why not be a missionary?

Flocks by night

(December 1995)

If you've had the good fortune to grow up on a farm, big or small, there are some things that have become a part of you. You have an instinct that will tell you till the day you die where you are likely to find wild strawberries in July, hazelnuts in October, field mushrooms after summer rain, blackberries in September. You know the names of trees and bushes, you distinguish easily between the green growing thing to be protected and kept for food, and the weed or poisonous item to be rooted up and eliminated. You have a feeling about approaching weather. You have a friendly understanding of the ways of your all-time friends, the animals. You have ... you have ... well, maybe call it a kind of subliminal *hearing* ... which the town-bred do not know.

Like the rare and memorable morning when I woke up in that hour of the first subdued light when the city was having its only moment of silence ... and knew by certain instinct that this silence was charged with something different. It couldn't be ... but it had to be ... the silence of a moving flock. And I got out of bed and looked down in joyous unbelief from my high window on a street and square awash in an ocean of sheep, waves and torrents of them, filling the carriageways and swarming on the footpaths, padding along without a single bleat. Out front marched the big gaunt figure of the shepherd. His two dogs away at the rear had little to do, for there were no stragglers. There was a clear conspiracy between shepherd and dogs and sheep to snatch the momentary lull in the traffic and get to new pastures by this strange short cut while the going was good.

You think that's fanciful, don't you? You should have seen that shepherd, such a total alien among traffic lights and circumscribed living. You should have seen the stride of him, seen the arrogance, totally unconscious, of a man sure of his values, sure about what is important and what is not. You should have seen the sureness of those sheep, hurrying along behind him, and *his* sureness that they were following him! You should have seen him, later, sitting down in the deep grass in a huge field on the city outskirts, eating his peaceful breakfast while the flock settled down and the dogs, at their posts, rested wide awake, chins on their front paws. You could have put that man in charge of the government.

It is the nearness of Christmas, of course, that has got me thinking about shepherds and remembering this particular shepherd who chanced to pass under my window one memorable dawn. There is a rather wonderful panoramic crib with life-size figures in a mountainside Franciscan shrine I sometimes visit, and the lighting is programmed so that each scene in the Christmas story is strongly illuminated in turn while all the rest remain in relative shadow. You have the Holy Family in their separate cave with ox and ass and with even a little fire flickering; and the Magi have a corner, and Herod's soldiers are tearing lovely little fat Holy Innocents brutally from desperate mothers, and Rachel is in the left foreground bewailing her children, while in the right foreground Joseph and Mary are setting out for Egypt, leaving a cheerfully gurgling little stream behind them as they head for the desert. There is where the lighting sequence begins again ...

Up on the heights at the back the shepherds come into brilliant relief. The sheep are all around them and the star swings high in the sky above, and you see the flight of angels, not quite alighting, but standing on air a little above the ground, and the artist has somehow managed to put joy and urgency into their whole demeanour as they pour out their tidings of great joy. 'This day is born to you a Saviour who is Christ the Lord in the City of David ... and this shall be a sign for you ... you will find a babe wrapped in swaddling cloths and lying in a manger.'

As the shepherds' field now dims and the nativity scene is picked out with its own bright illumination, you find yourself filling in the incidentals: the multitude of angels filling the sky and singing *glory*, the shepherds setting out for Bethlehem and finding exactly what had been promised, with the ox and the ass and the little fire flickering. And now you have been through the whole story over and over again. What stays with you as you go away is the sequel the crib could not show you ... 'how the shepherds returned glorifying and praising God for all they had heard and seen ... and how they made known the saying which had been told them concerning this child.' (What a missionary tries to do, in fact!)

Why not be a missionary?

When something like the moonflower happens

(January/February 1996)

An African colleague of mine has one of those clever little cameras with a flash that never fails and a lens that zooms in and out making thin buzzing noises. It is greatly to his credit, I think, that when I asked him to climb up on a very high wall and take a photograph for me in the dark, he hesitated not at all, nor looked at me strangely; he just went and did it. A day or two later, he gave me the picture ... of a flower blooming in the night. If the mail and the editor and the printers all do their stuff, it should be on the page with this piece of writing. I hope it excites you to wonder and delight, as it did me.

So what is all this about? Fundamentally, I suppose, it is about reputation, and how people perceive you. Coming from a green land, but living mostly in the smog-and-concrete heart of cities, I have some kind of inner need for honest clay and growing things, so flowerpots, watering cans and the debris of balcony gardening tend to be part of my living environment. A while back I mentioned to a friend that I could not find petunia seed in the local garden centres. The word spread like wildfire. Suddenly I had a reputation as a petunia maniac – and enough of the seed to sow a five-acre field. Another time it was onions. And once, because of loose talk, I had a half pound of turnip seed I did not know what to do with, along with a guilt feeling about wilful waste. Kind people jump to conclusions and disregard essential reality. But I cannot make a small farm out of a few terracotta pots and clay bought by the kilogram.

Ah, but then a miracle happens. Three different little packets of seed reach me from a kindred spirit near the Gulf of Mexico. I stow them away so carefully that I later cannot find them, but when I *do* eventually, the packets contain a smelly wet mush, heavily mildewed. I plant this stuff, with no hope, and forget about it. And then one night, in a warm October, high in the branches of the only tree there is room for on a bit of roofspace, I get the glow of something strange and wonderful. Can it be? – it's got to be! – a moonflower? Creamy, fragile, wide open face blooming in the night, so breathtakingly, heartbreakingly beautiful. And it is gone in the morning. There are three two nights later, and then two singles, with just one last one almost ready to open.

Well, the weather changes, a frigid northeasterly blows, the promise wilts on the stem and that is that. Now, please, everybody, don't send me moonflower seeds. I have the wrong climate, and I'll save the seeds from this year's freak success anyway. Besides, I have no means of knowing how much joy of this kind the soul can stand. I don't want to find out.

What I *would* like to know is why God made flowers that bloom only in the dark when nobody can see them. But then, of course, *he* can see them, and they must certainly glorify him by just being what they are. And this suggests all kinds of little parables about the marvellous people who live saintly lives in total obscurity, and you or I could name twenty with no smallest difficulty. Likely enough, your own name could be added to their number.

Meanwhile, I do the routine bitty tasks that fill a priest's days and often part of his nights, and I give, I hope, generally, the proper attention to the fundamental items which account for my *being* a priest; and then, the incidental bits of plant culture, weather watching, experimental cookery, computer exploration, and such like, serve well enough for mental hygiene. Overall, there is fairly solid contentment. When something like the moonflower happens, it becomes clear that joy is never far beneath the surface and prayer is likely to break out. And that's the honest truth.

Why not be a missionary?

The bits of being good
... one bit is being kind

(May 1996)

I am thinking of a long stone stairway in the sun, a stairway with many, many steps, climbing up to the top of a town called Coimbra, and at the top is some sort of touristy square in the middle of a university, and a bar on the edge of it with a wide view. I came down all those steps in a group of holiday-makers, and sat on a warm wall, and heard a little girl suddenly gasp – 'my camera!' – and she took off, back up all those steps, at speed, with her doting father a few paces behind, but gaining; and we all *hoped*. The camera had been a present shortly before, and it was new, but worse, it contained all the records of the previous days of foreign travel, and this was disaster. We waited, as the forenoon ebbed away, with varying degrees of patience or impatience, and some no doubt reflected on the featherheadness of the young, and the sun was warm and pleasant to sit in. When the pair rejoined us a long time later it was not by way of the steps, but by way of a police station where they had made the lengthy declarations required by insurance companies. They were crestfallen, and putting a brave face on it. We all shared the gloom of the moment. We drifted on down the hill, re-planning the day.

It was exactly then that I learned something which fixed all this positively and forever in my – well, in my *conscience*, I think. The girl's mother leant towards her there walking down the middle of the wide road. She said: 'I know just how you feel.' Nothing more than that, nothing at all dramatic or emotional, and no particular emphasis, but to me it seemed the essence of comforting. It said: 'Don't feel isolated; we've all done things just as stupid and often stupider; you belong with us.' It was solidarity, compassion, a miracle of tact. It was kindness out of a very loving heart. The response was instant and evident and inevitable.

There are kindnesses that you can never forget. It is many years now since I came down to that wide estuary on a motor cycle and saw the once-a-day ferry I had been racing to catch already well out from the jetty and making her turn for the run upriver. I heard good-humoured taunts from the more punctual passengers who knew I was stuck for twenty-four hours. But then I heard the bells ring in the engine room and watched in disbelief as the captain manoeuvred the five-hundred-ton ship back to the slipway to pick me up. He need not have and he probably should not have, and maybe it could happen only in Africa. But I still pray for that great black gentleman in the spotless naval whites who made his own compassionate decisions about when the book should be thrown away.

There was, as everybody knows, a wedding in Cana of Galilee, and a great lady there recognised a human crisis, and did the only thing she could think of to fix it, and put the clock forward with fearless trust in the rightness of what her heart prompted, and saw the water turn into wine.

Another great lady, and this one unmistakably of easy virtue, saw me come up a mud bank one day, drenched and shivering after a river crossing, and in the goodness of her good heart gave me a drink of firewater out of a bottle she had, and I bless her to this day.

And I could go on telling you stories like this, but there is no need. You are well able to find your own instances where a glorious bit of the gospel is put into practice: 'Be compassionate as your Father is compassionate. Do not judge, and you will not be judged yourselves. Do not condemn, and you will not be condemned yourselves. Grant pardon, and you will be pardoned. Give, and there will be gifts for you: a full measure, pressed down, shaken together, and running over …'

Here is what I really want to say: All my life, people have been telling me to be good. It began with my parents, and it went on through school and seminary, and the literature proposed for my reading, and the sermons I listened to and the torrents of exhortation poured out in the councils and synods and encyclicals and instructions. All aimed at me and flowing over me – and sometimes even getting through and reaching me. Be good, they all say. Well, even a backslider like me can try, but being good is such a large order. When they say (and they sometimes do): *be kind!* I recognize that this is one of the bits of being good. A place to start. Something I can possibly *handle*. And if and when I manage to achieve it, I'll know I'm most of the way there, because *kindness marks* anybody as being in the right camp.

Why not be a missionary?

The extra mile

(June 1996)

They must have known it was deadly dangerous for him to set foot anywhere near their home, but when Martha and Mary sent their anguished message to Jesus about their brother's illness, they quite evidently expected him to take instant action. They *knew* he would come. He had a very special reason for disappointing them, as we know, and he more than made it up to them afterwards, but it seemed totally out of character; it was not a bit like him, taking several days to move when someone appealed for help. And these were very close friends. Even with total strangers reporting the illness of a relative, his normal and predictable style was, *I will come and heal him;* and it did not matter at all that a long journey was involved. His style was to say ... *Yes, of course, be healed, be comforted* ... and it was expected. It is disbelief rather than reproach that rings in the identical greetings of the two sisters when he finally made it to Bethany: *If you'd only been here, Lord* ...

There was consternation in the camp down beyond the Jordan when he belatedly announced that he was going to Bethany. It was dangerous. It was foolhardy. It was asking for trouble. They were out for his blood, didn't he realise? The apostles were serious. The way the climate was over there, they really expected to be in grave danger just by being in his company anywhere near Jerusalem. They went with him anyway. Regardless of anything that happened later, this must never be forgotten. They put their lives on the line that trip.

I was reminded of this by something my confessor said to me this morning. He likes to throw in something that may prod me in the general direction of goodness, and today the message was: 'You know, a priest is not aiming to do just the minimum; nothing is good enough in his case but the utmost possible he can manage; that must be always what he is reaching for ...'

It set three videos going in my maverick imagination. The first one – you'll laugh – showed the two simple women that somehow got into an Irish lesson long ago: one left the other home after a visit, and then the other one left the first one home, and then they could not stop; they kept going back and forward all night, doing the polite thing. (There was a term in Irish for them or for what they were doing, but darned if I can remember it.)

My second video was John F. Kennedy making his inauguration speech, and though the 'ask not …' passage may sound a bit clichéd now, it was exciting and inspiring enough then when the world was young and had a dream of Camelot. Ask not what your country can do for you, but rather ask what you can do for your country.

The third video is running all day, on and off. It has been running really, I suppose, since the first day I heard it. The script is by Matthew, otherwise Levi. It shows somebody turning the other cheek. It shows someone running after the bandit who has stolen his overcoat, offering him the jacket as well. It shows someone going an extra mile after the mile he had not wanted to go in the first place. I suppose everyone has many a time run his own version of the same video, because the story is so outrageous that it excites the imagination … as well as afflicting the comfortable.

You can look in my direction and be sceptical. You can wonder if you are hearing alright, or whether we are on the same planet. You can point an accusing finger at all the things I am that I shouldn't be and at all the things I am not that I should be, and at all the things I do – or don't do – that I shouldn't or should (or am I confusing you?). You are welcome. I willingly acknowledge all the shortcomings and all the shortfalls; and I really can claim that I know a lot more about both than you do. I'll tell you one thing, though. I'm a priest, and I am staying with it; I am a missionary, and I am staying with that too; and if you are interested enough to want just one reason, I give you this one, without arrogance or apology: it is just that I have – in common with the other priests I know – some kind of notion I want to walk that extra mile. You might do worse than fall in with us.

Why not be a missionary?

Enough reality

(September/October 1996)

Zapping with the sound off. Channel One, Two, Three, and the forty-seven others always available, night and day, Sundays and major feast-days, and all the ordinary days of the week. Animated animals never seen on land or sea, talking heads, posing bodies, exploding fireballs ripping great apartment blocks to shreds, violent encounters with fists and weapons, copious spillings of blood, enormous, enormous destruction, then car chases, guns and silent screams and articulated trucks a mile long taking flight from clifftops, and slapstick, tired comedy, precocious children artificialised by over-exposure in the ads. And the video clips, flip, flip, flip, with so many clever images coming so fast, so many messages overlaying one another at such speed, that you are suddenly uneasy, and about to switch off. What – if anything – is all this doing to the set of my mind? How much of this rubbish can the spirit of man tolerate?

And then into all the craziness there quietly situates itself the totally unexpected very out-of-place picture of people lying in two concentric semi-circles on a large carpet, and while you count them the zapper clatters to the floor, and there are twenty-six. Out of the over-populated ether you have plucked by chance – off what modem or satellite who can tell? – the image of a *live* ordination ceremony. From the heart of triviality, the flimsy depths of artificial joy-making, there has emerged – in gob-smacking contrast – something so startlingly *real* that it finishes the zapping session quite abruptly. Your idling mind, out of gear from the passivity of the past minutes, comes sharply to question: What is this? What's going on here?

You should know – for, nearly two-thirds of a lifetime ago, you were part of something identical. You lay on the floor like the twenty-six in this bit of studied liturgical mime, dramatically pledging all your being, all your years, few might they be or many, to a risk-laden dream, to an ideal almost beyond believing, to a mystery and a marvel called the priesthood that you were certainly ready then to live for and to die for, and who might venture to say what exactly bore you along to that hour and moment! A man named Peter once stepped out of a boat on to the heaving waters, and it made all the sense in the world to him. It was a bit like that. A damfool adventure, some might say, but there was no reproof for Peter's foolhardiness, only for his loss of nerve. This was your life, your gift, your decision. Doubt was the one thing there was no room for.

You know, of course, my new brothers, where you are going, what you are doing, what is expected of you, what you must become? No doubt they have mentioned to you the concept of the *alter Christus*, of your being – you, mind you! – *another Christ?* You have surely read and heard and wondered about acting, as you will – and must – *you* – *in the person of Christ?* (stepping into his shoes, or having him step into yours – what difference? – to do the things he does, the things he can do only because you are there). You are familiar with the notion of pasturing the flock of God, of being a good shepherd, of being custodian and dispenser of grace? You have some grasp already maybe of what the Eucharist is, and is going to be, in your life, all your life, all your days? You've certainly pondered the words of the Vatican Council's decree on the priesthood: 'In the mystery of the Eucharistic Sacrifice, in which priests fulfil their greatest task, the work of our redemption is being constantly carried on …'? And it is not news to you that 'the world which today is entrusted to the loving ministry of the pastors of the Church is that which God so loved that he would give his only Son for it'?

That very world, my brothers on the TV screen, is your baby! I don't mind telling you, mawkish though it be, that I look on you with huge affection. I know what is driving you. I've been there. I've gone on from there, sure, and failed so many ways, and know there is far to go and the night not far away. But there you are, the twenty-six of you, sharing the dream, stepping cheerfully out on the heaving water. Think what your fearless faith is doing for mine! Hear my song of thanks and praise for the *reality* you represent and stand for and stand over!

Why not be a missionary?

Fr Michael Glynn

Michael Glynn, September 1973

Fr Michael Glynn

(November 1996)

'Father Glynn was a wonderful priest and person – kind, open, zealous, intelligent, sensitive,' wrote Archbishop John Foley, President of the Pontifical Council for Social Communications. 'In the Council, his own office became the center for the daily tea break, because he was so gracious and hospitable. He loved the world of the missions, especially Africa, where he had served. He was an inexhaustible font of information about those involved in the work of communications, especially in missionary lands.'

Fr Michael Glynn gave almost all his life as a priest to communications, more especially to the written word. After ordination in 1948, his first assignment was to Calabar, Nigeria, where he worked in St Theresa's Press as editor of *Catholic Life*. He was twice editor of *Africa* magazine (1952 to 1964 and from 1969 to 1970). From 1965 to 1968 he was communications secretary in the Catholic Secretariat, Lagos, Nigeria.

Fr Michael's first assignment in Rome was to FIDES news agency at the Congregation for the Evangelisation of Peoples in 1970. He then worked at the Pontifical Council for Social Communications from 1971 until 1993. For a number of years during that time he was secretary to the late Bishop Agnelus Andrew, OFM, who was Assistant Director of the Council.

'Father Glynn served as an official for the English-language section of this Council,' wrote Archbishop Foley, 'he followed with particular care the work of Unda, the international Catholic association for radio and television, and of Multimedia International, and the work of communications in Africa, Asia and Oceania and in his own Ireland and in Great Britain. He also compiled the *Communications Directory* this office published for the Catholic communicators of the world. He was an excellent writer and often prepared supplementary materials to accompany the World Communications Day messages of the Holy Father. The Holy Father honored him with the cross *Pro Ecclesia et Pontifice* and with appointment after his retirement as a consultor of this Council.'

'When Mickey retired in 1993,' wrote Fr Ned Carolan, OMI, a

friend from his early days in Rome, 'he proceeded to do a renewal course in the Redemptorist House in Dublin, hoping to go back to Nigeria, where he had worked in the earlier years of his ministry. That was not to be! Mickey was assigned to Rome again, this time as Procurator General for Kiltegan. Mickey loved Rome. He probably would have loved any mission to which he was assigned. He loved people and they loved him. During his long years in Rome, he was host to hundreds of visitors (maybe even thousands): missionaries on their way to and from Africa and elsewhere, student priests of Kiltegan preparing their degrees at the Roman Universities, relatives and friends, his own and those of his colleagues. Then, there were his many friends in Rome. Mickey was always ready to throw a party – often doing the cooking himself.'

Fr Cosmas OkeChukwu-Nwosuh, a member of the Nigerian Missionary Society of St Paul, was one of the many missionaries who experienced Fr Michael's friendship. 'Mike loved life and joyfully lived it well as a priest,' wrote Fr Cosmas. 'There was always a hearty feeling around him that seemed to proclaim "Life is gift to be celebrated!" Mike always had positive things to say about people, especially his fellow priests. But more than that he prayed for them. He prayed for many but hung on the wall of the sacristy the pictures of those to be specially remembered. Most were his fellow priests. Some of them are alive and well; some alive but sick, and others dead but never to be forgotten. It was his habit, as we prepared for Mass, to make comments concerning the various individuals. Thus, he issued me an invitation to pray with him for them. He routinely changed the pictures so as to give everybody a share in his prayers. Despite their race or status they were all to him, brothers and sisters. As I often watched him celebrate the Eucharist, I found myself repeating, "There ought to be nothing mechanical about the celebration of the Mass." He was never in a hurry to get it over with.'

Fr Michael always had time for people. 'Newcomers to Rome were met at the airport and given an introduction tour of the city,' wrote Fr Ned Carolan. 'Mickey kept up-to-date with events and happenings, cultural and entertaining, just so that his visitors could enjoy them. There were certain things which were basic: the Papal Audience, a visit to St Peter's, a visit to the shrines of St Francis, especially Assisi and Greccio. All visitors had that routine to go through and, under Mickey's guidance, they did so gladly and joyfully.'

Old friends, like Mary Taylor, had much to celebrate. 'I first met Michael on the first of January 1959, when he invited me to afternoon tea in Hope Castle, Castleblayney. I found myself on the two o'clock bus bound for Castleblayney on New Year's day, wondering what I was going to talk about until the next bus departed for Monaghan at five o'clock, but in fact with all the chat I nearly missed the nine o'clock bus. My last memory of him was a big hug and goodbye at Rome airport on the twelfth of May 1996, when my husband, Chris, and I came back from another wonderful, fun-filled, if sometimes hair-raising holiday with him – driving up the coast of Italy through the French Riviera and on to Orange, from where we explored Avignon, the Camargue, and especially Chateau-neuf-du-Pape, and all it had to offer. He was in wonderful form, ready for anything, and any attempt to offer a helping hand on steep hills was greeted with: 'I'm not a geriatric yet!'

'The friendship we shared in the intervening years has helped me through all of life's ups and downs – from the end of my teens, into my working life, into love and marriage and children – to the threshold of grandparenthood; and suddenly the unthinkable has happened and he is gone from us. Nobody ever thought of Michael as old, he was always there, welcoming visitors to Rome, travelling the highways of the world on his missionary endeavours, or the byways of Ireland keeping in touch with his friends, rejoicing, empathising, affirming, encouraging everyone, and enjoying life to the full.'

'I remember how important his prayers and his daily Mass were to him. His fidelity to these absolutes in his life have been an inspiration to me for as long as I've known him, and they never changed. No matter how urgent the meetings, how heavy the schedule, how enticing the party, how important the deadline, how long the journey ahead, Mass and the Office came first. We joined hands with him many times around altars, in places as diverse as our family dining-room, convent chapels, even the occasional hotel bedroom; but the most memorable must surely have been when our whole family marched himself and Uncle Joe (Taylor) to the top of a mountain in Connemara one windy September day to concelebrate Mass for my Dad's anniversary (and we had to hold on to the altar cloths to stop them taking off for America). The same evening, we all went to a medieval banquet to celebrate our daughter's twenty-first birthday: but somehow both feasts were all part of the same Eucharistic Banquet, where past and future, the sad and the glad, earth and heaven merged, and the mystery of the kingdom of heaven is now made sense for that moment.'

'Coupled with this fidelity was his sense of wonder at all of God's creation. But he showed the same sense of wonder at the marvels of God's creation that came to him through modern technology too – like his computer (and all the possibilities it opened up for the benefit of humanity); and he firmly believed that if Jesus had come about his Father's business on the threshold of the twenty-first century, he too would be on e-mail!'

'The memories of Michael are woven into every phase of my life, but more especially in the latter half of it, when he became a huge part of our family. Whether it was baptising one of our children, riding a crazy pirate ship in the funfair with them, celebrating birthdays and anniversaries; or visiting ancient monuments, exploring a champagne cave, eating gourmet meals in a restaurant with the obligatory panoramic view, or sharing a bag of chips by the banks of the Corrib, it didn't really matter what we were doing, when he was there, we celebrated just being – and we always had fun. And that's how I remember him – my friend.'

Michael was born to Elizabeth and Andrew Glynn in Taghmon, Mullingar, Co Westmeath, in 1922. He was one of a family of three girls and two boys. He was educated at Loughagar National School, and St Mary's Christian Brothers' School and St Finian's College, Mullingar. He was one of twenty-seven to come to St Patrick's Missionary Society, Kiltegan, in 1941.

After ordination in 1948 he was appointed to Calabar Diocese, Nigeria. He became editor of *Catholic Life* shortly afterwards and the written word was part of his apostolate thereafter. 'Writing is a lonely kind of job – not much dialogue about it,' Fr Michael once wrote to Fr Jim Cantwell, 'so you just hope you are reaching someone, but you seldom know for sure. It's a kind of act of faith most of the time.' Fr Jim from Swadlincote, England, knew Fr Michael through his writing and was in Ireland on the fourteenth of August for the burial of his friend. His parish bulletin contained the following tribute:

'Somebody once wrote, "I cannot get used to this vanishing trick my friends have taken to playing." Fortunately my own friends have not yet on the whole, started to play it. But my heroes have been doing so for a long time now, and the latest was last month, when Fr Michael Glynn ... died suddenly in Rome ... You in middle years and beyond will remember Fr Glynn. He was among the greats as a writer or, as he might describe himself, a chiseller of words. For forty-three years he wrote a monthly feature *Why not be a Missionary?* in the St Patrick's Missionary magazine, *Africa*. There should be bonfires on the surrounding hills for a man who wrote so much; he wrote of saints and made them human; he wrote of God's love for each of us and whatever he wrote was always filled with true Christian hope and assurance. He used to talk of the marvellous people who live saintly lives in total obscurity and you or I could name twenty with no smallest difficulty. Likely his own name could be added to their number.'

'Mickey's death was a shock to all of us who knew him,' wrote Fr Ned Corolan. 'Yet, in retrospect, he could have enjoyed that too. He was a media man. He kept up with the times, not only in being well informed, but in technology too. He mastered the use of the computer and he had just linked up with the Internet and examined his mailbox every day. It was another instrument in his service to his brother missionaries. They were always foremost in his thoughts. He had probably settled down to watch the afternoon news bulletin on television on the fifth of August 1996, when God sent his final message.'